I WANTED WINGS
The autobiography of Leonard M. Thompson

To Mr & Mrs King,
Enjoy your time here in
Hope Town & we look forward
to your return.

Warm wishes,

Chris Thompson

Abaco, Bahamas

Atlantic

Ocean

Walker's Cay

Grand Cays

Strangers Cay

Carters Cays

Fish Cays

Great Sale Cay

Moraine Cay

Allans-Pensacola Cay

Little Abaco Island

Spanish Cay

Powell Cay

Manjack Cay

Green Turtle Cay

Norman's Castle

Whale Cay

Great Guana Cay

Sand Banks /
Treasure Cay

Man-O-War Cay

Marsh
Harbour

**Great
Abaco
Island**

Hope Town

Elbow Cay

Tilloo Cay

**Grand
Bahama
Island**

North Bar
Channel

Great Abaco
Beach Hotel /
Boat Harbour

Little Harbour

Mores Island

Cherokee Sound

Gorda Cay

Crossing Rocks

| 0 | 10 | 20 |

nautical miles

Sandy Point

Hole-in-the-Wall

I WANTED WINGS
The autobiography of Leonard M. Thompson

Leonard MauriceThompson, O. B. E.

cover paintings by Jim Marsh

White Sound Press

First Edition
Second Printing

Cover illustration - A Grumman Goose in Hope Town harbour c. 1948. Painting by
Jim Marsh, my nephew, son of my sister Velma and best friend Alf Marsh.

ISBN 0-932265-38-3

Library of Congress Catalog Card Number:
95-061829

Published by

White Sound Press

Exclusively distributed in The Bahamas by

Leonard M. Thompson
P. O. Box AB20419
Marsh Harbour, Abaco, Bahamas

Voice: 809 367-2678
Fax: 809 366-0434

To Mary
for all the love and happiness
we have shared and all the hard
times we have been through together

Leonard

COMMONWEALTH OF THE BAHAMAS

No. _____
IN REPLYING PLEASE
QUOTE THIS NUMBER

OFFICE OF THE PRIME MINISTER
P.O. BOX CB 10980
NASSAU, N.P., THE BAHAMAS

FOREWORD

It gives me great pleasure to pen a foreword to Captain Leonard M. Thompson's memoirs; a colourful vignette of Bahamian history.

A nation's history is made up of the lives and achievements of its people. Captain Thompson, a proud Abaconian, presents in his life's story, an interesting window into a time in The Bahamas when young Bahamians were formed the old fashion way; through hard work and sacrifice.

Captain Thompson's account of his trials and accomplishments as he sought to become a pilot, serve in the Canadian military and fight fascism on the European front during World War II, provide another poignant reminder of how unassuming persons, from small colonial territories, made a difference to that major international effort in the middle of this century.

The challenges he met in carving a role for himself in the evolution of our country from colonial times to the development of internal self government, majority rule and eventually political independence, provide an important insight into the political development of a most interesting Bahamian citizen.

Hubert A. Ingraham
Prime Minister

July, 1995

Leonard Maurice Thompson is one of the most remarkable Abaconians I have ever known and I rate him in the top twenty Bahamian males of the century.

My association with him dates back to 1954 when he flew into Cherokee Sound in a Grumman Goose at 2:00 a.m. in order to save my mother's life by air lifting her to the hospital in Nassau.

Since 1977 we have been exceptionally close, having fished, played, travelled and argued together.

The story of Captain Thompson's life from childhood days in Hope Town through his early manhood years, his war experiences, and his contribution to the growth of aviation in the Bahamas as well as his contribution to the economic and social growth of the country, especially Abaco, makes interesting and exciting reading.

These memoirs will be found in hundreds of homes, as well as in libraries and museums, for generations to come, as a testimony to this outstanding Bahamian.

Truly Leonard M. Thompson is a remarkable man.

Patrick J. Bethel

Marsh Harbour, Abaco, Bahamas
July 1995

Captain Leonard Thompson, O. B. E. has lived an amazing life!!!!

I have always loved and admired the man. He is very sincere, down to earth and has great love for his family, his fellow man and his country.

In 1939, at age 22, he left his country and family to join the Royal Candian Air Force to fight in World War II. Six years later, in 1945, he returned home after being shot down over Germany and having spent over a year as a prisoner of war.

He underwent an ordeal and having survived it, he proved equal to all of life's challenges.

As his life unfolds in this autobiography you will see the qualities of a true national hero. He is a modest, generous, and most unassuming role model.

Thank you Captain for taking the time, in your vintage years, to record your marvelous life story. It is a shining example to all.

Sincerely,

Basil T. Kelly

Table of Contents

Leonard M. Thompson

I WANTED WINGS!

While in a POW camp in Germany a friend asked me why I joined the Royal Canadian Air Force. My reply was that I wanted wings. This apparently prompted the caption on this sketch he made.

CHAPTER 1

CHILDHOOD YEARS

I was born in Hope Town, Abaco, Bahamas, on 17th June 1917, the second son of William Maurice Thompson and Lena Muriel Thompson (nee Albury). My parents wasted no time in extending the family and I eventually had six brothers and one sister: Hartis, Roscoe, Chester, Maurice, Harvin, Vernon (Joe) and Velma.

My father was a seaman who spent most of his time away from home. He was a descendant of one of the early settlers who arrived on Harbour Island from Bermuda in the mid-sixteenth century. *The History of The Bahamas House of Assembly* by Harcourt Malcolm shows that the first Assembly comprised 27 members. Six were from Eleuthera and six from Harbour Island, two of whom were William Thompson Sr. and William Thompson Jr., the first of my ancestors to arrive in the islands.

William Thompson was buried on the Eastern Parade in Nassau. His tombstone still stands and bears this epitaph:

Remember, Man, as you pass by -
As you are now, so once was I.
As I am now so you shall be.
Remember, Man, eternity.

My mother's ancestors were among the earliest Loyalists who settled in Abaco shortly after the War of Independence between the United States and England. The story goes that there was an over-abundance of beautiful girls in the Abacos and a shortage in Harbour Island. Eligible men left Harbour Island for Abaco to find wives and

1

my great-great-grandfather, William Thompson Jr., was among them.

I can still remember my great-grandfather Joshua Thompson, who was in his late 70s when I was a little boy of seven or eight. I often went to his sail shop with my father to watch as they sewed the canvas and told their stories of shipwrecks and lost treasure.

Norman Albury of Man-O-War Cay remembered my great-great-grandfather, who was known as Old Keg. According to Mr. Norman he came by this nickname when he and a friend had gone turtle hunting on the east side of Hope Town. In no time one was spotted and over the side he went to catch the turtle. His partner waited and waited in the boat, scanning the sea all around, but all he could see was a barrel drifting a long way off. In desperation he decided to return to the village for help.

The search party was led by Joshua who, when he heard about the barrel, stopped and turned back. "That's no keg, that's my father out there!" he exclaimed. "Don't you know he can stay underwater as long as a turtle?"

My earliest childhood memory is of my first day at school. There was a commotion and the mother of Joe Russell, one of my schoolmates, walked in and grabbed him by the arm and marched him out of school. Other mothers came for their children and soon I was the only student left. "All the others have gone," said the teacher, "you may as well go too."

At home I discovered that a doctor and nurse had arrived on the island to vaccinate all the schoolchildren against smallpox. The rumour had spread among the students that the vaccination was very painful and could cause one's arm to rot off. But in the end we all lined up and everything must have turned out well for I have never had smallpox and still have both arms.

Hope Town was a fun place in which to grow up. There was always so much to do. Everyone had a small sailboat and we learned to sail at an early age. I eagerly looked forward to treasure hunting trips with members of my family. Spanish galleons had been wrecked on the coral reefs in the area and there were many stories about treasure being buried on remote cays. These hunting trips led me to beaches that had rarely felt a footprint in their sand.

At the age of eight or nine I persuaded my mother to let me go turtle watching one night. She reluctantly agreed, provided I was back by midnight.

During the early part of the summer huge female loggerhead and green turtles would crawl up on the beaches just above the high tide mark, dig holes and lay dozens of eggs. The eggs were considered a delicacy and eagerly sought after.

At about ten o'clock I started out alone to walk a long stretch of deserted beach. I soon realised I would have to pass the graveyard in the dark. Brave as I tried to be, my boyhood imagination took over and, chased by a ghost, I found myself well on the other side of the graveyard. There was no way I would pass that graveyard again in the dark. Around midnight I could no longer stay awake so I dug a hole in the sand and piled seaweed and scraps of driftwood around as a lean-to to keep the wind off.

I must have fallen asleep quickly for the next thing I remembered was the sound of loud voices from a search party my mother had sent for me. They were busy digging in the sand trying to locate the eggs of a turtle that had dug its nest almost on top of my lean-to. I think I was more up-set about sleeping through the chance to see a turtle laying eggs than I was about the inevitable punishment that awaited me when I reached home.

Much of my life revolved around school and one of my favourite teachers was a redheaded Englishman named George Morley. Later on in life we became very good friends and remained so until his death, but while I was in school he often had good cause to apply his bamboo cane to my rear end.

Mr. Morley loved to shoot and he kept his shotgun behind his desk. Sometimes my friends and I would excit-edly point through the open shutters and describe a great flock of ducks that had just flown over heading for the pond. It worked every time. Mr. Morley would delegate the senior

3

monitor to take over the class, grab his gun and run. He never did catch on that we arranged these frequent 'holidays.'

One day we were given a real holiday to observe the first sea plane to land at Hope Town. That day, I am sure, affected my future life.

A crowd gathered and grew until everyone in Hope Town–man, woman and child–was lining the harbour beach, staring into the sky. Suddenly the call went up: "There it is!" And there it was, taxiing slowly into the harbour. The plane had landed outside and no one had seen or heard it until it was almost to the beach where we all waited.

The plane had been chartered by J.W. Roberts, a Hope Town boy who had become very successful and owned a large lumber mill at Norman Castle on the west coast of Abaco. He had brought in a doctor to attend his mother, who was very sick at the time.

The pilot was Captain A.B. Chalk, an early pioneer of aviation in The Bahamas. His company, Chalk's Airline, still flies to the islands and is now operated by Paradise Island in Nassau. There and then I decided that some day I would become a pilot like Captain Chalk.

Years later my dream came true and on numerous occasions I flew out of his home base near the Biscayne Bay causeway in Miami. Captain Chalk and his wife Lily, who ran the ground operations of the airline, became two of my dearest friends and I affectionately called them A.B. and Mammy. The Bahamas, and Bimini in particular, lost two great benefactors when A.B. and Mammy passed on after giving a lifetime of service to the islands.

The Methodist church controlled the majority of people in Hope Town and, as a result, there was never a dull moment. There was constant feuding amongst the leaders of the church about such trivial matters as: "Pearson pumps the organ every Sunday. It should be Jasper's turn this week;" "Mrs. M. raised the hymns for the past month. It's time Jenny had a turn. At least she can carry a tune..." These petty matters set family against family and sometimes they would not speak to each other for years.

The Methodist ministers were treated like royalty and loved every minute of it. Any other denomination that tried to establish itself on the island was run off. This happened to Dr. Kendrick, one of the finest Christian gentlemen to ever arrive in The Bahamas. He and many members of his flock, who were born and had their homes in Hope Town, were intimidated to such an extent that they were all forced to flee, move to Green Turtle Cay and start their lives all over again.

Dr. Kendrick was the only medical practitioner in Hope Town for many years. He had developed a herbal treatment for skin cancer that was very successful. As his reputation spread, patients from all over The Bahamas came to him for treatment. Unfortunately, when he passed away the formula for the treatment was lost forever.

My father spent most of his life in sailing ships. He was one of the first Bahamians to obtain a Master Mariner's Licence from the Board of Trade in London, which included a Navigator's ticket. When he was home, which was mainly during the hurricane season, he taught navigation. I often sat in on his classes and had a good grasp of the subject from an early age. This came in very handy many years later when I joined the Royal Canadian Air Force and commenced training as a pilot.

The family moved often between Nassau and Hope Town during my early years and where we lived depended on where my father was sailing from at the time. For instance, when he was hauling lumber to the Gulf ports of Florida and Jamaica or Cuba from Norman Castle, we moved to Hope Town. Sometimes we made a trip with him, which we all enjoyed.

Getting to Norman Castle to meet Dad presented quite a problem for my mother, but as a young boy I looked forward to the trips as they provided many opportunities for exploring new and unfamiliar areas.

We never had an accurate time of arrival for Dad because he might have encountered head winds or no winds at all. Unloading the lumber at the final destination might have taken longer than anticipated. There were no telephones on the island in those days.

Whenever my mother was given an approximate date of arrival by telegram or a passing boat captain we would leave Hope Town on a chartered sailboat with a small cabin to protect her from the sun and rain. We usually left early in the morning and headed for Sand Banks Creek, about 20 miles north of Hope Town where the island is only half a mile wide. A road led to the west coast where a shallow draught boat would be waiting to take us on the final leg of our journey to Norman Castle, about 10 miles further north.

If Dad was not there waiting for us we would walk a short distance to Mrs. Sarah Hodgkins' plantation and stay with her until Dad's arrival. Aunt Sarah, as we called her, was originally from Green Turtle Cay. She had moved to Sand Bank Cay with her husband many years before and had built a comfortable home in a plantation with many tropical fruit trees. After her husband passed away she continued living there on her own. She always seemed happy to see us and we loved her like family.

On one occasion we were there for two weeks before Dad finally picked us up. It was during this time I discovered the most beautiful beach in The Bahamas, located on the east side of Sand Banks Cay. I never forgot those happy days exploring the area. I even fantasized about building a great resort beside the long crescent of perfect beach now known as Treasure Cay.

During Prohibition in the late 1920s to early 1930s, all alcoholic beverages were banned from entering the U.S.A. As a result, bootlegging of liquor from The Bahamas to the eastern seaboard from Florida to New York became an immensely profitable venture. The sale and export of liquor from The Bahamas was perfectly legal. Entry into the States was the illegal part and most transactions took place outside the three mile limit.

To take advantage of the situation the government of The Bahamas imposed an enormous tariff on all landed liquor and thus filled a public treasury that had for many years been quite dry. Quite a few Bahamians made fortunes, mostly Nassau merchants who were able to obtain exclusive agencies for top brands. Nassau became an immense warehouse for trans-shipment to Bimini and West End and then to the States. Small, fast powerboats would make two or three delivery runs a night to inlets on the east coast of Florida. These were mostly manned by Americans but the longer hauls, such as to New York, were handled by Bahamians–like my father, and some Canadians as well.

At this time Dad was the captain of a three masted vessel called the *Alma R.* He made several runs to New York where he would anchor outside the three mile limit and do business. Boats of every size and description would come and tie alongside the vessel and make their purchases. For fear of hijacking, nobody was allowed on board. The buyer would call out his needs and be given a price. A bucket was lowered and the full payment placed inside. Then the goods would be passed down. The bottles were packed in sixes, each covered with a straw sleeve and sewn up in a burlap sack. These could be easily passed or thrown down to customers in the small boats.

After a few close calls from the U.S. Coast Guard, including an occasion when the *Alma R* dragged anchor into the three mile limit during a heavy blow, Dad decided to install a large diesel engine. He had inspected a sailing ship owned by a friend in the same trade that had been converted to auxiliary power and was impressed. He decided to try and talk the rest of the shareholders into the conversion.

I will always remember his discussion with my grandfather, who was definitely against such a move. Engines gave more trouble than they were worth, he argued. They wouldn't be around for long, just you see. The smoke dirtied up the sails and decks and the smell made decent sailors sick.

This type of thinking resulted in the death of the sailing ships from Abaco and Harbour Island. The failure to convert their vessels in order to compete with the new steam ships was a grave mistake on the part of Abaco seamen and boatbuilders. It brought about the migration of Abaco's more ambitious people to Nassau and Florida.

Within a few years Hope Town, a thriving community of over 2000 people, dwindled to a population of just over 200 by the late 1930s.

Dad won his argument and the engine was installed. On the second trip thereafter the *Alma R* encountered gale force winds and rough seas prevented the small boats from making contact. The ship's New York agent provided a pilot and encouraged Dad to move inside to a protected bay that was well off the beaten track.

Against his better judgment, Dad agreed. He moved in after dark and for several days there was brisk traffic–too much, perhaps. A message arrived from the agent saying the Coast Guard had been tipped off and Dad should leave at once.

Unfortunately, the tide was low and before it was high enough to cross the bar and enter the safety of the three mile limit the lookout announced the imminent arrival of the Coast Guard.

They were trapped and knew it. Dad called a trusted crew member, a black man from Green Turtle Cay known as One-Eyed William Bowe. They packed all the proceeds from the expedition into a pillowcase and put it in with dirty laundry. Dad knew he would be arrested and imprisoned, but crewmen were usually released and given a reasonable amount of time to leave the country. His charge to William was to deliver the money intact to my mother.

There were more than twenty crewmen on board. The fact that Dad entrusted the money to One-Eyed William was a measure of the high esteem and love Dad had for him.

The Coast Guard boarded and, sure enough, Dad and the engineer, Cyril Albury, of Harbour Island, were arrested. The rest of the crew, including William, were released and made their way to Miami then Nassau. One-Eyed William handed the money over to my mother without a cent missing.

After a few days the New York agent arranged to pay Cyril and Dad's fines and they were released. The *Alma R* was sold at public auction and shortly thereafter was back on Rum Row again. A few years ago Cyril's son Edward, a dear friend, gave me a painting of the *Alma R* that I treasure.

My father captained this Hope Town-built three-masted schooner which he eventually converted to diesel. Note the smoke stacks. Named the *Alma R.*, it was confiscated during prohibition for bootlegging off New York and was sold at a public auction. This painting was given to me by Edward Albury whose father was chief engineer.

An aerial view of my birthplace and hometown–this is Hope Town Harbour. Later in life I would land the Grumman Goose and Widgeon in the empty harbour.

CHAPTER 2

GROWING UP IN HOPE TOWN

In a short period of time fate had dealt the people of Abaco a series of blows–literally–in the form of four major hurricanes. Back in those days hurricanes were not named but called after their years. Abaco suffered in 1926, 1928, 1929 and 1932. Prior to this, Abaco had been spared for over fifty years.

After the 1932 hurricane few houses were left standing in Hope Town and many of the sailing vessels were lost, along with their crews. The largest vessel ever to have been built in Abaco, *Abaco Bahamas*, was at its moorings west of Parrot Cays near Hope Town, where there was deep water. During the hurricane it broke away from its moorings and drifted five miles, ending up 100 feet inland at Murphy Town. When you consider the boat drew ten feet empty, you can appreciate the power of a hurricane.

A few years later she was sold to a boat builder who dismantled the *Abaco Bahamas,* took her to Harbour Island and built two freight boats from her, the *Isle of June* and the *Betty K I.*

Much the same happened to the beautiful colonial style homes that were destroyed. The remains were used to build smaller versions of the original Hope Town homes.

Many lives were also lost in Cherokee Sound when a large commercial fishing boat went down with its crew as well as several smaller boats. Some were later found miles inland from Morgan's Bluff, Andros. You have to experience a hurricane to appreciate the devastation left in its path.

During the depression of the early 1930s, right after Prohibition ended in the U.S., my father was without a ship and a job so he decided to try his hand at sponge fishing. He found a small sloop, the *Primrose,* hired a crew and arranged for a six week trip. He took my brother, Roscoe, and me on as members of the crew for the summer with a promise to my mother he would bring us back in time for the new school year.

The crew consisted of a cook and two men to a dinghy. For this trip we had three dinghies, the most we could accommodate. The senior man for each dinghy was called the "hooker." He searched the sea bed through a glass bottom bucket for sponge and when he spotted one he called instructions to his partner, the "sculler," to keep the boat above the sponge. In the meantime the hooker would position his sponge hook that was attached to a pole almost 30 feet long. The hook would be maneuvered under the sponge then an upward pull would set the hook and the sponge would be brought on board.

I acted as sculler for my father, who did the hooking. Roscoe, who was eleven at the time, was the cook (with a little help and some planning from Dad). The other members of the crew were all close friends from Hope Town who thought sponging would be a great adventure. Sleeping accommodations below deck were crowded and malodorous so I always slept on deck, no matter how bad the weather.

We made our headquarters at Sales Cay where there was a protected anchorage and a good supply of fresh water for washing clothes and bathing.

Our day began at first light when we sailed to the chosen area, eating a light breakfast on the way. Once in the dinghy Dad would start his search for sponges while I sculled according to his directions. This was difficult on days that were breezy or when there was a strong current.

Around midday the mother ship sailed nearby and we would pull alongside. Roscoe would pass us each a heaping plate of food and, without leaving the dinghy, we would wolf the food down then get back to work.

Near the end of the day we would arrange to be near our headquarters. The day's catch would be put ashore to dry and later put into a corral we had built in the water. After about a week of soaking the sponges would be individually pounded with a 'bruiser,' a type of mallet, and the dark skin washed off. When they were clean and dry they were stored in a shelter to keep them from the weather.

On Sundays we did no sponging but set aside time to do our cleaning and laundry. After that we just lounged around.

It was on just such a day that I was ashore exploring an old abandoned camp site. It began to rain so I went into a little thatched hut to wait out the storm. Later, when I came back to the boat, Dad offered me his hand to help me out of the dinghy and onto the stern of the *Primrose*. Suddenly he dropped his hand. "Stay where you are!" he shouted. "Don't dare get on board. You're infested with crab lice!"

Dad went into the boat and came back with a kerosene lamp. He joined me in the dinghy and took me to shore. There my clothes were discarded and I was thoroughly inspected from top to bottom. The only area affected was the bridge between my eyebrows. I was scrubbed so hard with kerosene oil I thought my skin would come off. When Dad was satisfied with his scrubbing I was allowed back on the boat.

At the end of the fourth week the staples like rice, beans and flour were getting low so we decided to head back to Hope Town. From there the sponges were sent to Nassau to be auctioned off at the Sponge Exchange that was owned by two Greek families.

Roscoe and I anxiously awaited our share of the proceeds. Imagine my disappointment when I received a mere sixteen shillings. It was explained to me that the net proceeds from the sale of the sponges was used first of all to pay for the groceries and provisions. The owner of the *Primrose* received one-third of the balance. The rest was divided into shares with two shares for the hooker, one for the sculler, and one for the owner of the dinghy.

While it was true that no one had a great deal of money in those days, no one ever went hungry and everyone was happy. As kids we played marbles, flew kites, and spun tops that we made from lignum vitae. Our favourite ball game was rounders, an early form of baseball. But our favourite activity was sailing.

By age eleven I would take off with friends in our sailing dinghies and take a trip through the cays. Sometimes

This boat, *The Offshore*, was built in 1960 with mahogany I hand selected in British Honduras. It was the boat of my childhood dreams.

we went as far as Walker's Cay, the most northerly island in the Abaco chain, a round trip of some 200 miles.

Our first day's sailing would take us to our camp site at Allen's Cay, where there was a well with fresh water. We would usually find a palmetto covered shade where we would set up housekeeping. We referred to this site as our Ranch. When the mosquitoes came out, we would anchor our dinghies off from shore and sleep in them. We were tough and sleeping on the bare boards was no problem.

We showered by drawing a bucket of water from the well and having a partner pour some water over our heads. After soaping, the partner would pour more water to provide a rinse-off. I always liked to be second or third in line for these showers as the first bucket of water was always full of little wriggly tadpoles that got entangled in my hair.

When we tired of our first ranch we would move on to the next at Sandy Cay, near Double Breasted Cay, just south of Grand Cay. On our return journey we would gather whelks, catch a turtle or two and find some seabird eggs.

To ensure that the eggs were fresh, we carried a bucket of sea water and dropped each egg in. If it sank it was fresh, and if it floated, it was returned to the nest.

CHAPTER 3

TO CANADA

After graduating from High School I had several jobs around Nassau including a year at the Royal Bank of Canada where I soon discovered there was no future for a Bahamian. I decided to quit when I found that a Canadian, trained by me, was paid double the salary I received. In addition he was paid a living allowance and given a free apartment.

Shortly after leaving the bank in early 1937 I persuaded my friend Charlie Collar, a US Naval Pilot and later the pioneer founder of Bahamas Airways, to take me on as an apprentice pilot for the great sum of one pound ($4.80) a week. My duties consisted of cleaning and washing down the two aircraft, one a 9-passenger twin engine Douglas Dolphin and the other an 8-passenger single engine Loening, both amphibian.

When a charter came up I would refuel the aircraft and load the luggage. At the destination I would drop the anchor and unload the baggage. Whenever there were no passengers on the return flight I would get the chance to fly the aeroplane under the supervision of Capt. Collar or Capt. Leon Brinks. Several nights a week I would join two pilots and the mechanic, Bob Addison, to practise Morse code which was the only means of communication with another aircraft in those days.

After a while I became quite good at sending and receiving Morse code messages. This worked to my advantage because Capt. Brinks could not get beyond five or six words per minute and was rather reluctant to call our Pan American Airways base station. As a result I became his ever ready anchor boy and he would occasionally let me do landings and take offs.

Now and then he would make a bad landing. Whenever that happened he would step smartly into the passenger cabin and with a straight face would say, "Sorry, folks. Sorry about the landing–I'm teaching the young boy how to fly!"

Some time later I discovered why he made the occasional poor landing. He always travelled with a vacuum flask which he claimed contained coffee. Whenever I asked to share his coffee he refused. "Bring your own. This is too strong for you," he would declare. Indeed it was, as I found out one day when Capt. Brinks had to go ashore in one of the Out Islands. The moment I saw him get onto the dock I opened his flask, took a good swallow and started choking. The flask contained undiluted gin! After this I noted that his bad landings invariably followed frequent nips of "coffee."

At the outbreak of World War II in September 1939 I thought I knew so much about flying that the Royal Canadian Air Force would welcome me and my skills with open arms. How wrong I was, as I would find out later.

After weeks of talking about the war, four of my closest friends and I decided we would take off for Canada and join the Royal Canadian Air Force (R.C.A.F.). I sold my motor bike and boat and received a few donations to make the grand sum of $300. I also had the offer of a free ride on a small freight boat to Miami.

When the day of departure arrived I discovered that my friends had suffered cold feet and decided not to go to war. One of them, Garth Johnson, did go later on. He paid his way to England and joined the R.A.F. as pilot of a Lancaster bomber. He and his crew were killed over Germany. The other three remained in Nassau and by the end of the war, each had made a fortune.

In Miami I spent a few days with Harold Key, a friend of the family. He convinced me that the cheapest way to get to Canada would be by Greyhound bus to Ottawa via New York.

The driver of the bus was a young man of my age who introduced himself as Walter McMillian. He pointed

This portrait was taken of me in 1939 when I was 22 years of age.

out places of interest on the way and kept us all together at food and bathroom stops. There were no toilets on buses in those days. Long before we reached New York we had become fast friends and he suggested that I stay over with him for a few days before going on to Ottawa.

His mother welcomed me warmly. She became concerned, however, when Mac (the nickname I gave to Walter) expressed the desire to go with me and join the R.C.A.F. as well. At that time many Americans went to Canada to join the Canadian forces as the U.S. had not yet entered the war. Mrs. McMillian had her way and Mac saw me off on the bus to Ottawa to continue my journey alone.

Six months later he did join the R.C.A.F. and trained as a pilot. Just before graduation he was killed instantly when he accidently stumbled into a spinning aircraft propeller. Long after the war was over Mrs. McMillian came to Nassau to visit with us and we kept in touch until she passed away a few years ago.

I had chosen Ottawa as my destination because I knew very little about Canada at the time and thought that the capital was the obvious place to go. On arrival I was surprised to find that most of the people I tried to get directions from at the bus terminal did not appear to be friendly. I was finally directed to the local Y.M.C.A.

The manager there told me he had no rooms; they had all been taken up by young men from Bermuda and the Caribbean. I turned away dejected and homesick. The Bahamas seemed a million miles away. I wondered if I had not been too hasty in coming to Canada. To make matters worse, I had spent most of my money in New York.

I was standing on the fringe of a group of young men having a spirited discussion when one turned to me and said in a distinct Jamaican accent: "I suppose you are here to join the R.C.A.F. as a pilot? If so, you are in for a surprise, we have all been here for weeks. Every day we go to the Recruiting Centre and it's always the same story: 'Come back tomorrow.' The only way they will take you now is if you are a university graduate or a famous hockey player." I was sadly lacking on both accounts.

The Jamaican was Brian Clackon from Kingston. I confided in him that I was damn near broke and had nowhere to go. A born leader, he took the matter in hand and arranged with the manager to have a cot put in his room for me. He had done much travelling, so different from the rest of us who had never been away from home.

There were ten young men in our little group, all from the Islands: Barbados, Bahamas, Bermuda and Jamaica. Early the next morning we all walked to the Recruiting Centre and I filled in my application forms. For the first of many times I was given the standard instruction: "Come back tomorrow."

After two weeks of this I pleaded with the recruiting officer and pointed out that I was broke and would have to cable my family for the price of the bus ride back and boat to Nassau. He must have felt sorry for me because instead of "Come back tomorrow" it was "Come back this afternoon."

That afternoon I was taken to a room where a large display of aero engine parts and accessories was laid out on tables. An R.C.A.F. sergeant pointed to the various items and asked what they were named and what function they performed. He must have been satisfied with my responses because he nodded and said, "I can see that you have worked around aircraft."

Then it was back to the recruiting officer who told me, "It might be months before you can join as air crew. I suggest you join today as a mechanic and later on you will have no trouble remustering as a pilot." Like a drowning man clutching to a straw, I readily agreed and signed up. The next day I said goodbye to Brian and the boys and was on my way with a travel voucher to Toronto Manning Depot.

Three months later Brian's persistence paid off. He trained as a pilot and on graduation was posted to Coastal Command and stationed in Nova Scotia for the duration of the war.

One night five years after the war was over I was pilot on a DC-3 aircraft heading for Miami when I heard a B.W.I.A. pilot calling Miami Tower. I immediately recognised the Jamaican accent as that of my old friend who had helped me so much in Ottawa. We made arrangements to meet at the airport.

Brian had become the Chief Pilot of B.W.I.A. and I was Chief Pilot and Manager of Bahamas Airways. We spent the rest of the night reminiscing as neither of us was scheduled for an early morning departure. From then on we often met in Miami and have kept in touch throughout the years.

These gentlemen were leaving Nassau for England to join the Royal Air Force. Back row: Garth Johnson, George Mosley and Warren Lightbourne. Each graduated a pilot and was killed in action over Germany. Front: Hartis Thompson, R.A.F. ground staff and Philip Farrington, R.A.F. pilot instructor.

CHAPTER 4

ST. THOMAS, ONTARIO

I arrived at Toronto Manning Depot late in the evening and was assigned the top position of a bunk bed in a large auditorium. There were several hundred young men all standing by their beds waiting to be checked in.

Shortly after the lights were turned off someone called in a loud voice, "Anyone here from the west?" It was followed by "Down with the west!" and "Down with the east!" and within a few minutes a pillow fight started and bunks were turned over. The Air Force Police arrived and order was quickly restored.

I spent a week in Toronto Manning Depot and was outfitted with a uniform, shirts, shoes and a greatcoat. The uniforms came in two sizes: too large and too small. My uniform jacket came well below my knees and on my first pay day ($1.75 per day) it was off to the tailor for a proper fit. We were inoculated for every contagious disease known and, it seemed, for some that were not known.

My first "short arm" inspection came as a complete surprise to me and was extremely embarrassing. Sixty of us were lined up and told to strip. The doctor and his orderly walked down the lines, stopping at each airman with the instruction, "Cough, skin it back and squeeze." Just down the line from me the doctor stood in front of a tall skinny guy for a rather long time. "Congratulations, you lucky man," he said finally. We all peered around to get a look at the specimen in question. One airman piped up: "No wonder he's so skinny, having to carry that load around all the time!"

Shortly after this I was posted to St. Thomas Technical School, a newly-established small station near London, Ontario. There were two courses, Air Frame Mechanic and Engine Mechanic. I was assigned to the latter. When I had my first appointment with the Commanding Officer I told him I had been promised on my day of enlistment that I would be able to remuster as Air Crew shortly after joining up. I would be a far greater asset to the war effort as a pilot, I tried to convince him, but he cut me off. "Get out. Don't waste my time. You are dismissed."

A NOTABLE FAMILY RECORD

My brothers and I were sometimes known as the "Fighting Thompsons" because four of us went off to fight the war. This is a clipping from one of the Nassau newspapers. From left to right, Leonard, Maurice, Chester, and Hartis.

    During my second month at St. Thomas I received a telegram from Mac in New York telling me my father was critically ill in a New York hospital. I went straight to the C.O.'s office and passed him the telegram with a request for leave. I was stunned when permission was denied. "The U.S. is not in the war," he explained by way of excuse. "If you showed up in the States in uniform you would immediately be interned."

    I asked my Canadian friends about the location of the nearest border crossing and found out it was Fort Erie, just across the Niagara River from Buffalo. A bridge connected the two and there was a port of entry on each side. I boarded a bus for Fort Erie at close to midnight. It was a two hour drive and when I arrived I changed into civilian clothes, left my uniform in a locker and crossed the bridge.

It was very quiet, no traffic at all. On the U.S. side an immigration officer sat all alone in the inspection building reading a book. I had to speak up in order to get his attention. Foolishly, I decided to be honest with him. I showed him the telegram and told him my story. He was very sympathetic but refused to let me enter the country because I was a Canadian serviceman. I turned away with thoughts of returning to the Canadian side and swimming across.

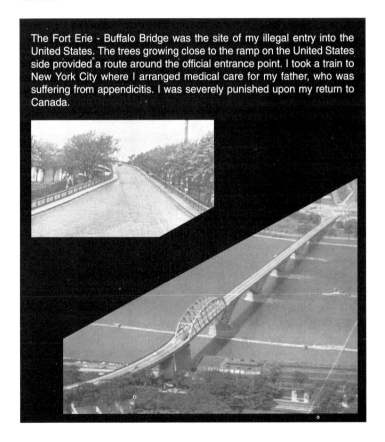

The Fort Erie - Buffalo Bridge was the site of my illegal entry into the United States. The trees growing close to the ramp on the United States side provided a route around the official entrance point. I took a train to New York City where I arranged medical care for my father, who was suffering from appendicitis. I was severely punished upon my return to Canada.

Halfway back I stood watching the strong Niagara current swirling around the pilings. I changed my mind about swimming. Instead, I headed back towards the U.S. check point hoping the officer on duty would still be engrossed in his book and I would be able to sneak by unobserved.

On the way back I noticed for the first time that large trees were growing close to the bridge on the U.S. side. A wire fence ran from the river to the check point and beyond this was a road. Within seconds I was over the bridge, into a tree and onto U.S. soil.

To my dismay I discovered the fence was much higher than my fleeting glance from the bridge had led me to believe. Also, the top angled inwards and was covered with sharp barbs. By the time I had climbed the fence and jumped to the ground my hands were pouring blood and I had a large rip in my pants.

It was four o'clock in the morning and not a soul in sight. I walked several blocks expecting at any moment to be arrested. I came across a man who directed me to the railway station. There I washed the dried blood from my hands and made myself halfway presentable. I checked out the train schedules then sent a telegram to Mac to advise him of my arrival time in New York.

Once on the train a very nice black conductor had me sit in the toilet while he mended my pants. When he had finished you could barely see where they had been torn.

Mac met me at the station and told me that Dad was in the paupers' ward of the hospital. Unless we could remove him there was little hope he would survive. What to do? While racking our brains I remembered Col. Lansing, an American who lived in the New York area. Dad had worked for him for years as captain of his yacht. Mac contacted Col. Lansing by phone and I started to explain the situation in some detail. "Never mind that," he interrupted. "Just tell me where your father is."

When Mac and I arrived at the hospital we found that Col. Lansing's doctor had already made arrangements to have Dad moved to a private room. When we contacted him he told us he had examined my father and that he was, indeed, in critical condition and would soon have died if not treated. He had a ruptured appendix and peritonitis had set in, making a blood transfusion necessary. Fortunately, both

Mac and I had the same blood type as Dad so that problem was solved.

With my father now in good hands, Mac told me the full story. Dad had been hired to deliver a yacht from Nassau to New York. Shortly after arriving he had passed out in the marina office while trying to contact Mac. He had been rushed by ambulance to the hospital while the marina office contacted Mac at home. He had immediately rushed to the hospital where he found Dad in a large room surrounded by many half-dead people, all waiting their turn to see a doctor. He realised he had to get Dad out of that room and find proper treatment for him if he was to survive. That was when he had contacted me.

I stayed in New York until Dad was well on the way to recovery then headed back to St. Thomas to face the music. I noted at the Buffalo check point that the walk-through gate was locked and had to be opened from a look-out station near the main office, so the fence had been the best way in after all. This time I had no problems with U.S. or Canadian authorities. I changed into my uniform at Fort Erie bus station and caught the next bus to London.

On arrival at St. Thomas I was arrested then threatened and ridiculed by the same Commanding Officer who eight days earlier had refused me permission to leave. My punishment was twenty-four hours pack drill and confinement to camp for the remainder of my training.

Pack drill consisted of marching from the guard house to the administration office two hours every day for twelve days. This was done with full pack: winter clothes (including long johns and overcoat), fifty pound back pack, and a rifle.

I was the first to receive such a punishment on this new station and I was subjected to many snide remarks from passing airmen. For my part, I thought I had got off with a light sentence. But no matter how severe the punishment might have been, it would have been worthwhile. Dad was alive and well.

CHAPTER 5

MY MARY

On completing the course and graduating as a fully qualified aero engine mechanic I was posted to No. 7 R.C.A.F. Pilot Training Station at Fort McLeod, Alberta. My initial duties consisted of flight line services, refuelling aircraft and having them ready for instructors and pilot trainees. What a heartbreaking chore to watch the pilots take off and land while I seemed no nearer to realising my dream of becoming a combat pilot.

Our station was located about two miles west of Fort McLeod, at one time a famous outpost for the Royal Canadian Mounted Police. A small town of some two thousand people had grown around the fort and hitching posts and water troughs still stood in front of a small hotel.

The nearest large town was Lethbridge, thirty miles away. It had a population of 16,000 people, half a dozen hotels, restaurants, bowling alleys, beer parlours for men only, and–last but not least–lovely western girls.

I soon discovered the people of Alberta were considerate, friendly, warm-hearted people, unlike the Canadians I had met in Ottawa. The Ottawans reminded me too much of some of the arrogant English colonial officials I had known in The Bahamas.

Every other week we were allowed a 48-hour pass. The moment we had our pass in hand we would walk the short distance to the highway to hitch a ride and usually the very first car would stop. On many occasions we were picked up by folks who would drive miles out of their way to deliver us safely to our destination.

Once, a pickup truck stopped with a farmer, his wife and two young children. When I told him we wanted to go to Lethbridge he said, "Sorry, we're heading home to Pincher Creek. Why not come with us and we will bring you back Sunday afternoon before your passes expire." It was over fifty miles to their home. My buddy, Alf Marsh, and I piled in with the children and what a great time we had that weekend. We arrived back at the base just before deadline, five pounds heavier and bearing a box filled with goodies.

I fell in love with the people of Alberta and I often think of them with fond memories. Over the years I have made many trips back to Alberta and I am pleased to say time has not changed these wonderful people.

My closest friend in the R.C.A.F. was Alf Marsh from Hamilton, Ontario. We met in St. Thomas and were transferred to McLeod together. It was through him I met the girl of my dreams, in a rather unusual way.

Alf had a friend called Jack Steel. Jack visited our corner of the barracks one day and we sat around chatting. As usual, the conversation got around to girls. Jack passed around a photo of a girl he had met recently in Lethbridge. I was impressed.

Later I persuaded Alf to get her name and phone number from Jack. Her name was Mary. I called her, pretending to be Jack, and we made a date to meet at the bowling alley. Then my conscience got the better of me and I confessed I was not Jack but would still like to meet her. She agreed, on the understanding that if we did not like each other we would go our separate ways with no hard feelings.

When we met and shook hands the sparks between us were so great it was a wonder the bowling alley didn't catch fire! Just one year later we were married.

It wasn't that easy, however. Just as my Nassau friends had developed cold feet about going to war, I grew apprehensive about going to the altar. As the date drew nearer I began to miss weekends in Lethbridge. Obviously, Mary suspected something. Alf returned from a weekend on his own and brought an ultimatum from her. The girls were going to hold a shower for her on the following Saturday. "If I don't see you on Saturday I know you will leave me stranded at the altar," she wrote. My fate was sealed. How could I disappoint her after that?

More than fifty years have flown by since that day and I have never once regretted showing up for the shower ... or the altar.

Mary and her family immigrated to Canada from the Ukraine in 1932; she was raised on a farm but at sixteen moved to Lethbridge. She worked for a wonderful Jewish couple, Abe and Ida Davids. They were affectionately called Cappy and Mammy by their numerous Air Force friends, who always knew where to go for a great home-cooked meal.

The Davids had four children, two daughters and two sons: Evey was about Mary's age; Doreen was small and cuddly and I nicknamed her 'Suzie Q'; Dave was away in the Air Force; and Hymie, who married Mickey, a sweet girl from Boston, during the war. She had a prodigious memory.

Mary and I considered Hymie and Mickey our dearest friends. They spent many vacations with us in later years and we always hated to see them head back to the cold. Mammy was the greatest cook there ever was and Mary learned a lot from her–I have the ever-expanding holes in my belt to prove it! Cappy had a very dry sense of humour and was very protective of Mary. During a family visit to Old Man River he called me aside and, with a serious look on his face, said, "Please be very careful and look after Mary. She swims like a *pibble*."

We were married in Lethbridge and the Davids gave a reception as if we were their own children. All of Mary's girlfriends were there, along with half the airmen from the base. Until then I had not realised how many friends I had on base!

I had never met Mary's parents, William and Anna Tofin, so a few weeks after we were married we drove to Olds, Alberta, where they owned and operated an 800 acre farm.

Imagine my surprise when we arrived at the farm to find the farmhouse surrounded by vehicles of every description: vintage cars, trucks, tractors and horse-drawn buggies.

This photo was taken at our wedding reception in Lethbridge by my R.C.A.F. friend from Fort Mc Cloud.

There were well over a hundred Ukrainians, Poles and Swedes present, and a party was in full swing. I was hugged and kissed by all the women–and how they could hug! Several times I thought I heard my ribs crack. Every man insisted on drinking a toast with me, each time with a new drink. By the time I had finished the last toast I was walking a few inches off the ground.

Mary arrived just in time to allow me to make a getaway to the house and up the stairs to bed. When I fell on the bed it seemed I would never stop falling. The cover on the bed was a thick homemade quilt filled with down. The next morning it took a while to figure out where I was. I felt I was in the middle of a cumulus cloud. What a hangover! I swore I would never drink again.

Early the next morning, my guardian angel Mary arrived and told me to stay where I was–the party was still going strong. I didn't need convincing. I settled back into my feathery cloud and cared less what those tough farmers thought of Mary's new husband.

Mary's parents were good, kind, hard-working people and I fell in love with them within minutes of meeting. They also had two daughters and two sons. Nelly was very like Mary. She went to school and worked in Calgary but came back to the farm to lend a hand whenever she could. The two boys, Sam and Andrew, had also moved to the big city but showed up on weekends and at harvest time. I had married into a lovely family.

Mary and myself on our wedding day on 8 October, 1941.

CHAPTER 6

INTO THE AIR

As the weeks and months went by, I constantly badgered the Padre, the Commanding Officer, and anybody else I thought might help my remustering to air crew. Eventually this paid off.

One day the C.O. called me to his office and advised me to be sure and read the Daily Routine Orders the next morning. I was waiting by the bulletin board when the D.R.O.s were posted. With great joy I discovered I had been approved for Air Crew Training. I would be leaving the following morning for Initial Training Wing in the University Building at Edmonton.

All air crew started at I.T.W. and were graded for various positions on the aircraft: pilot, navigator, gunner, bombardier or wireless operator. Airmen were then posted to special schools for further training. Upon graduation they usually went overseas to an Operational Training Unit.

Pilots had to undergo a very extensive and thorough course in navigation, theory of flight, meteorology and other related subjects. They were then tested and those who passed went on to Elementary Flying Training School. Those who failed were sent to either Bomb Aimer or Gunnery School.

Fortunately, I was one of the lucky ones and was posted to No. 5 Elementary Flying Training School at High River, Alberta. The school was right beside the Duke of Windsor's ranch. Our time was divided between ground school and flying. We trained in a very popular single engine plane, the Tiger Moth.

A good percentage of the trainees were washed out in the first few weeks. They either found out flying was not for them after all or became airsick during aerobatics. An airsick trainee had to leave the programme. Had it not been for a kind and sympathetic civilian instructor, Mr. Hawkey, I would have joined the ranks of those unlucky airmen.

In the Tiger Moth trainer the pilot and student pilot sat one behind the other. There were wing mirrors placed so the pilot could see what was happening in the rear seat. On this particular occasion I was in the rear seat behind Mr. Hawkey when we went through a series of steep turns, spins and slow rolls. I became nauseous and realised I was going to lose my breakfast. In desperation I slipped my cap from under my belt and unloaded into it, hoping I had not been observed.

The moment the wheels touched down I threw my cap and its contents over the side. After taxiing in and shutting the motor off I quickly jumped to the ground, hoping to get away before Mr. Hawkey could stop me. I wasn't fast enough. He called for me to stop, walked over to me and said, "Bahamas, you really want those wings, don't you?"

"Yes, sir," I replied.

"I believe your cap blew off. Go around to stores and I'll arrange for you to get another one."

I finally soloed and enjoyed all phases of flying, particularly aerobatics. While I was at the controls I was never sick.

I graduated with twenty-five of my class and we were posted to No. 10 R.C.A.F. Service Training School at Dauphin, Manitoba. There we had a more advanced ground school and flew in twin engine Cessnas in the middle of winter with temperatures that frequently dropped to 50 degrees below.

The Cessna cabins were heated directly from the engine through ducts. This worked fine until we lost an aircraft pilot instructor and student who were on instrument training. In order to block off all reference to the ground a black hood was installed around the pilots and over the windshield. The student pilot then had to fly completely by instruments. An investigation into the accident indicated that carbon monoxide gas had been trapped under the hood. After this, out came the hot air.

Navigating on cross-country flights in winter was quite a challenge. The ground was completely covered with snow so the usual references on the ground like rivers, lakes and roads were a blanket of white. We tried to find smoke from farm house chimneys then search for grain elevators, for they always had the name of the town painted on them in large letters. Then we tried to find the town on the map and adjust course.

After studying and flying all day I would walk into town across frozen snow drifts to a little upstairs bedroom that Mary and I rented from a wonderful old couple, Mr. and Mrs. Cox. They allowed us use of the kitchen and Mary spent all day near a big old wood-burning stove, waiting for me to return. Any food we wanted to keep frozen we just placed on the window ledge.

On one occasion I arrived home a little early. I expected to find Mary in the warm little kitchen but Mrs. Cox told me she had just gone to our room. I went upstairs and did not find her there. The only other place she could be was the bathroom. Wanting to surprise her, I entered the bathroom as soon as I heard her flush. There was Mary wildly waving her arms trying to disperse smoke from a cigarette she had just disposed of in the toilet. From that moment I knew I had lost the battle with Mary and her smoking.

I was not very good company for Mary in those days. The moment I finished eating I was off to the bedroom to study until well after midnight. I was determined to get those wings and learned to get by on four hours sleep a night.

After months of training, graduation day finally arrived. Even after my wings were pinned on by our C.O. I could not believe it. I kept looking at my left breast to make sure the wings were still there. I was posted overseas, along with thirteen of my class. Only three of us returned at the end of the war.

We were all given two weeks embarkation leave so I decided to take Mary to meet my family and return at the

I had just graduated as a pilot when this photograph was taken in 1942.

end of my leave. She fell in love with The Bahamas and, with a little persuasion from my parents, decided to remain in Nassau.

All too soon my leave came to an end and I headed for Boston. We thought we would be embarking from there but instead spent a week of close confinement with numerous lectures about security and German agents ready to contact U-boats the moment we sailed.

Then, with no warning and in the middle of the night, we were hustled out of our quarters and taken in closed trucks to the railway station. Within minutes of boarding we were on our way. Only the top brass knew where we were going and they were not talking.

After a long, tiring ride we arrived at the end of the line. We quickly transferred to buses for a short ride to the docks. There we boarded the *Queen Mary*. The rumour went around that we were in Halifax, Nova Scotia, and would be sailing some time that night.

We were packed like sardines down in the bowels of the huge ship. Although I was assigned a hammock somewhere I ignored that and went back on deck. Once we were under way the majority of the soldiers and airmen were taken with seasickness. Those of us with good sea legs roamed the decks for the short dash across the Atlantic. Fortunately for us, the *Queen Mary* was the fastest liner of the time and could easily outrun the German submarines.

CHAPTER 7

ENGLAND

When we landed at Portsmouth, England, in early 1943 we were taken by train to Bournemouth, a popular seaside resort. There we were billeted in a plush hotel which had been taken over by the Canadians as the R.C.A.F. Headquarters.

During my short stay there my brother Chester, who had joined the British Navy and was stationed nearby, came over by train for a brief visit. I walked with him back to the railway station and we had just entered the station gate when we heard low flying aircraft. I spotted two German FW 19Os heading straight for the station.

Luckily there was a water trough on a concrete stand nearby and I flung myself behind it. The area was strafed and I heard the noise of exploding bombs. When the sound of the retreating aircraft had disappeared I noticed that Chester was bent over beside me in a crouch.

"For God's sake, why didn't you get down with me?" I admonished him. "You could have been killed!"

"I did not want to get my uniform dirty," was his calm reply.

Shortly after this I was posted to an R.A.F. station at Church Lawford, near Rugby, for a Beam Approach Training course flying twin-engine Oxfords. All of the pilots in training were Colonials: Canadians, Australians, New Zealanders and such. All the administration, instructors and ground staff were English. Unfortunately there was a lot of hard feelings, mainly due to the superior attitude of some of the English officers which, unfortunately, reflected adversely on the many decent ones. These officers considered the Colonials inferior, over-paid and over-sexed.

Shortly after arriving at Church Lawford I had a taste of the arrogant attitude of one particular English officer. On Saturdays most of the trainees rode bicycles into Rugby for a pub crawl. Just outside the station were steep hills. We sped down the first hill in order to build up enough momentum to reach the top of the next one. On one occasion my cap flew off on the way down and I had to stop and pick it up and secure it under my jacket belt. Because of this stop I was not able to make it to the top of the hill.

I had just started pushing my bike when a man walked out of the woods and onto the road directly in my path. He was the typical snobbish Englishman–knickerbockers, cardigan, hat, swagger stick and walrus moustache. In a loud parade ground voice he snarled, "You are improperly dressed. Come to attention and salute your superior officer. That is the worst of you Colonials, you have no respect for your superiors. All of you need discipline."

I was so mad I came very near to striking him. Looking back, I am sure it was his age that held me back. He looked old enough to be my father. "Get out of my way before I knock you down," I warned him and continued on my way to meet my friends at our favourite pub.

When we returned later that evening there were several Military Police at the gate and I heard one of them say, "We are looking for the airman with 'Bahamas' on his shoulders." When I stepped forward and identified myself I was told: "You are under arrest for insubordination to a superior officer." I was hustled off to the station jail, not even allowed to go back to my room.

Next morning I was escorted by two M.P.s to a kangaroo court martial. To my horror the Presiding Officer, seated at a table and dressed in the uniform of a Squadron Leader, was the Englishman I had encountered on the hill. I later found out his name was Nicholas and that he was the Paymaster. He was flanked by four of his brother officers, all ground administrative staff.

I was not allowed to say one thing in my defence. When I tried I was shouted down by S/L Nicholas and repeatedly told I was an undisciplined Colonial who needed to learn respect for his superiors. I was sentenced to six weeks at Sheffield Detention Centre.

I was escorted there and closely guarded by two M.P.s who acted as though they expected me to make a break for it. On arrival in Sheffield I found that my punishment consisted of a tough commando-type training that started at five in the morning and ended well after dark. I then had to write a hundred lines: "I promise that at all times I will instantly obey without question any orders given by a superior officer." It was interesting to find that all the airmen at the centre were the hated Colonials–not one Englishman.

On one side of the detention centre was a barrage balloon repair centre run by the Women's Auxiliary Air Force. In a surreptitious conversation with members of this service we discovered they had been instructed not to talk to us as we were all dangerous, hardened criminals.

On return to Church Lawford I found out that S/L Nicholas resented having to pay Sergeant Pilots twice the

On my way to Rugby for a pub crawl some time before my problem with squadrant leader Nicholas and subsequent detention at Sheffield.

salary he personally received. This disparity in rates of pay led to much jealousy and hostility from the British servicemen, who were paid next to nothing compared to the Canadians and Americans.

I had a visit from a senior R.C.A.F. officer who told me they were well aware of the problems many Canadians were having with some of the R.A.F. ground personnel. He assured me my detention would be expunged from my records and at the end of my training I would be posted to an all-Canadian squadron.

A few weeks later I was posted to No. 23 Operational Training Unit at Pershore, Worcestershire. I was very happy to see the end of Nicholas and his cohorts. Shortly after my posting I was promoted to Warrant Officer First Class, clear proof that my personal record had been wiped clean.

It was the responsibility of a bomber pilot to personally select his air crew. On the first day at Pershore we all met in a hangar to find our navigators, wireless operators, bombardiers, flight engineers and gunners.

I struck up a conversation with P/O Harry Fewetrall, a wireless operator who came from Penticton, British Columbia, and had previously been a member of the Royal Canadian Mounted Police. He had a wife and daughter back in British Columbia. He seemed to be the nervous type but I was impressed with him. I invited him to join my crew and he agreed provided I would take his friend, P/O Hostetlar, as our navigator.

We found Hostetlar and I was pleased to find he had graduated top in his navigation class. Before joining the R.C.A.F. he had been a professor at the University of Toronto. He was still single despite being much older than most of the airmen. We set out to find the rest of our crew together.

The next to follow was a bombardier, P/O Cuff, who hailed from Newfoundland. He was single and had left college to join the service.

Then came Sgt. Merritt from Toronto as mid-upper gunner. He had left high school to join up and was the youngest of the crew.

Merritt introduced us to a friend from gunnery school, Sgt. Tarpley, who agreed to be our rear gunner. He was also from Toronto and single and had worked in a department store.

Last came Sgt. Lock from Manchester, England. He too was single and had worked as a mechanic in a car pool before joining up. He would be our flight engineer.

Part of my crew–Navigator Hostetler; rear gunner Tarpley; bomb aimer Cuff; wireless operator Fewetrell. Missing is engineer Lock and mid upper gunner Merrit.

The following day we commenced flying together and training as a crew in a large twin engine Wellington bomber. The first few hours was mostly familiarisation– circuits and bumps, single engine approaches and such. After this we were on our own.

We trained day and night, dropping dummy bombs and practising evasive action. This consisted of attacks by fighter aircraft which, instead of using live ammunition, tried to "shoot us down" with a camera synchronised with their guns. We had to perform violent manoeuvres to avoid their attentions.

We also gave the gunners practice by shooting at a drogue that was towed by a small single engine plane. We used live tracer bullets and the pilot was always complaining that the cable was too short. I did hear about one towplane that was hit; fortunately the pilot was able to bail out.

When we were not flying we attended ground school. We went through aircraft recognition, dinghy drill and parachute drill as well as attending lectures on escaping after being shot down over enemy territory.

We were scheduled for our first raid over enemy territory but instead of bombs we dropped propaganda leaflets. These operations were called nickel flights because in those days you could buy a small Canadian newspaper for five cents. The success of the operation was determined by taking a photograph of our dead reckoning position at a turning point half-way to the target, and a photo flash picture of the target area.

My first flight over enemy territory was in a Wellington bomber. We dropped propaganda leaflets over occupied France. Photo courtesy of Charles E. Brown.

We took off at midnight in a Wellington bomber, all alone on a four hour flight to Orleans, France. We saw no German fighters and very little in the way of flak or searchlights. With the help of our capable navigator we brought back two great photos of the turning point and target. All in all it was a beautiful flight that left me ill-prepared for what I would later experience.

A few days later we were given 48-hour passes with instructions to report to a Heavy Conversion Unit afterwards where I would be checked out in four engine Lancaster and Halifax bombers.

With my pass in hand I set off for London to meet up with Garth Johnson, my boyhood friend from Nassau, who was a Sergeant Pilot flying Lancaster bombers. We met at the West Indies Committee building which had been converted into a club for servicemen from our part of the world. Lady Dawson was in charge and really went overboard to make us all feel at home. This was always our first stop to pick up messages and mail.

It was great to see Garth again. We went out to explore London and soon discovered that in order to get into the best clubs it was necessary to become a member. This meant paying an exorbitant fee for a minimum of one year. This was a rough deal when more than half of the new airmen members would be dead or in a P.O.W. camp in a matter of months. In Garth's case, death was just a few weeks away.

All too soon we said goodbye with a promise to meet on our next leave. With just a few hours to spare I arrived at No. 1679 Heavy Conversion Unit located at Wombleton in Yorkshire. Luckily my training did not start until the following day. I was exhausted from lack of sleep.

After a short time with my instructor and flight engineer I was checked out in both the Lancaster and Halifax. The instructors were all veteran pilots who had completed a tour of thirty trips over enemy territory. When my instructor told me he would be getting out after the next landing as he felt I was ready to take my crew, I strenuously objected. I told him I needed a few more take offs and landings. "Look, you are not too bad," he told me with a weary voice. "You will be all right. But some of those smart-asses scare me half to death. I would rather be shot at over Germany than be an instructor." So off I went with my full crew, who little knew how terrified I was sitting at the controls so far off the ground.

We then trained as a crew on cross-country flights, making numerous practice bombing trips to designated target areas. After 24 hours I felt I was flying the aircraft, not the aircraft flying me. After a final check ride we were posted to an all-Canadian Squadron 6 Group 426 Thunderbird at Linton-on-Ouse, near the city of York.

CHAPTER 8

INTO ACTION

On arrival at the squadron my crew was given a short vacation while I completed two trips with an experienced crew over Germany. Two operations with a veteran pilot were deemed to be necessary for a new pilot so he would know what to expect and see how an experienced crew reacted when attacked by enemy fighters, flak barrages and searchlight batteries.

These two trips had to be made with a pilot having a minimum of ten trips (Ops) over Germany. Fifty per cent of all bomber crews went missing before their tenth trip. Occasionally a pilot would be so frightened on his first trip he would refuse to go on another Op. When this happened he would be charged with lack of moral fibre, stripped of his wings and rank, and assigned to ground duties. This seemed very harsh at the time but it was necessary to discourage others with similar ideas.

I flew my first trip with Squadron Leader Avant, one of the oldest and most experienced pilots in the squadron. As I later found out, we were given an extra-special meal before each Op. We then collected our flying gear: fleece-lined flying boots; leather flying helmets with built-in phone, mike and oxygen attachments; Mae West life jackets; parachutes and, finally, chest harnesses in which the parachutes could be quickly clipped on to. We emptied our pockets of all personal items and placed them in our lockers.

In the briefing room we discovered our target that night was the trainyards of Essen deep in the Ruhr Valley, Germany's largest industrial area. After the briefing we went outside to await our turn for the crew bus that would take us to our aircraft. When I thought no one was looking I tested my parachute harness to make sure it was not too tight. I discovered my trousers were too tight around the crotch and as I tried to adjust the harness S/L Avant noticed and said, "Relax, Bahamas–you will feel a lot better once we are airborne."

The bus arrived and took us to the aircraft. One of the crew placed his parachute on the ground and S/L Avant told him to pick it up. "The grass is wet," he explained, "and you may need your 'chute later on tonight."

Those that smoked lit up cigarettes, each man deep in his own private thoughts and apprehensions. The non-smokers like myself walked around the aircraft, a Lancaster, unable to stand in one place. Finally Avant announced it was time to enter the plane.

On arriving at my station I put on my mask and made sure the intercom and oxygen were plugged in and working properly. It was believed oxygen improved night vision so most crews started using it on the ground instead of waiting until we reached 10,000 feet when its use was mandatory. There was no proper seat for a second pilot, only a bicycle-type seat that was attached to the starboard side and folded out for use. The space that would normally have controls and a seat for the second pilot had been eliminated to provide easy access to a flight of steps which was used by the bombardier and nose gunner to reach the nose section.

Right on time a green flare was fired into the air, the signal to start all four engines. We taxied to the take off point and waited for our turn to take off. Seconds after we stopped a green Aldis lamp was beamed directly at our aircraft and we were off. We used every last foot of the runway and commenced a slow climbing turn around the aerodrome in order to gain a safe altitude before crossing the enemy coast. Strict radio silence was maintained on the outward flight in order not to alert the Germans, who were very good at monitoring our radio frequencies.

After we had reached our cruising altitude of 18,000 feet we passed near a large town, easily identified by its hundreds of searchlights criss-crossing the night sky like a giant octopus reaching out with luminous tentacles to catch its prey. Avant pointed out several blue searchlights which he explained were master beams, controlled by radar. Once a master beam fixed on a bomber all the other searchlights in the battery would zero in on the unfortunate aircraft. It was then almost impossible to get away before the orbiting German fighters arrived. With a full load of bombs it was very difficult to take evasive action. Sometimes bomber crews had to jettison their bombs in order to carry out violent corkscrewing manoeuvres in an effort to get out of the blinding searchlights.

As we flew deeper into Germany the flak became more intense. There was no way to get around it. It looked like a thousand fiery red tennis balls leaving the ground and heading straight towards us. The explosions shook the aircraft as if giant fists were pounding on the fuselage. Out of the corner of my eye I saw the squadron leader fighting the controls as we passed through the terrifying turbulence.

We saw three of our aircraft hit. Each plunged towards the ground in flames, followed by a huge explosion. I was sweating so badly I took off my mask for a second to wipe my eyes. I caught a good whiff of cordite from the bursting shells and hastily put it back on. After this experience I never took off my mask until we were safely on the ground.

As we approached the target area the navigator called the pilot to tell him the Path Finder Force would be marking the target with green flares in five minutes. Right on time the flares went down, lighting up the target as if it was broad daylight. An Australian voice came through the headphones: "Hello, main bomber force, this is Black Tie One. Aim your bombs fifty feet to the right of the green markers." Then the bomb aimer took over. "Hello, Skipper. We are coming up on target...Open bomb doors...Steady, steady....Right, right...Hold it!...Bombs away...Close bomb bay doors."

What a relief! Even the aircraft seemed to feel it and surged forward and upward as if saying: "Now I am rid of that monstrous load I am ready for anything."

The return trips to base were much easier than on our way to the target. The aircraft handled much better empty and evasive action kept us away from flak and searchlights. The duration of the flight was five hours. Nine of our aircraft failed to return. The crew bus picked us up after we landed and took us to the debriefing room. After debriefing we enjoyed a special breakfast of bacon and eggs. This was a treat as eggs were rationed and served after each flight to aircrew only.

I should mention more about the Path Finder Force (P.F.F.). This was an elite squadron made up of experienced crews and the latest navigation aids who flew fast Mosquito bombers or Lancasters. Their job was to mark the target with coloured flares just minutes before the main bomber force arrived. This was called Parameter bombing. They flew at very low altitudes so their losses were much greater than the main bomber force. When the target was covered by clouds the P.F.F. dropped parachute flares above the clouds as our aiming point. This was called Wanganui bombing. The names were given by the Royal Australian Air Force and adopted by the R.A.F. and R.C.A.F.

On March 30th, just three days after my first raid on Germany, I went on my second familiarisation Op to Nuremberg in a Lancaster with Pilot Officer Barry in command. The previous trip was mild compared with this nightmare. Looking back, it was the worst raid of the twenty-five I completed before being shot down.

There was a full moon shining and the German night fighters knocked us off as they pleased. The whole operation was a bad mistake made by the Big Wheels who ordered it. We lost 97 bombers that night. 500 young men were killed and 200 taken prisoner. This was the greatest one-night loss suffered by the Americans or British during the entire war.

My boyhood friend, Garth Johnson from Nassau, was shot down on this raid. He died along with all of his crew. Just a few weeks earlier we had enjoyed such a joyous reunion in London, making plans for all the great things we would do on our return to The Bahamas.

What a horrible waste of so many young boys' lives for so little return. The target was at the maximum range of the Lancaster, 1500 miles. As a result the bomb load was a mere 500 pounds with 15 cans of incendiary bombs and 2,250 gallons of fuel. All the P.F.F. were shot down before reaching the target area so we saw no markers. We dropped our bombs on fires we saw on the ground which could have been one of our own bombers shot down in the first wave.

It was the rule that gunners would report when they spotted one of our aircraft going down and the navigator would note the time and mark the location on his map. After numerous reports of aircraft going down on the port and aircraft going down on the starboard Skipper P/O Barry instructed the crew: "No more reporting. Keep your eyes open for fighters!"

We twisted and turned and performed evasive action all the way back across the French coast. On two occasions we were attacked by fighters. Thanks to the skill of the pilot and good eyesight of the gunners we were able to lose the fighters, but not before getting two hits in the midsection. I breathed a sigh of relief when the gunners reported all clear and prayed that the next aircraft they attacked would have a crew as alert as P/O Barry and his crew had been.

We arrived back at base just as the sun was rising, with twenty minutes of fuel in the tanks. I was so tired that when I climbed out of the aircraft my personal undercarriage, my legs, just folded up under me and I fell to the ground. I had to be helped to the crew bus.

That Op had been 7 hours and 50 minutes of hell. 781 Lancasters and Halifaxes had been dispatched on this raid. 55 aircraft turned back for some reason, mostly mechanical. 129 aircraft failed to return. 97 of them were shot down by German fighter planes.

After this Op it was announced that the German night fighters' great success was due to a recent modification of installing upward-firing cannons on the ME110s and JU88s, their top twin engine night fighters. These aircraft were also fitted with a new form of radar that could pick up a bomber from a distance of 15-20 miles. Prior to this raid the British had not been aware that Germany's radar capability had advanced to such a degree.

The German night fighter would pick up a bomber on the radar then overtake it from well below, out of sight of the rear gunner. The fighter would then climb up directly beneath the bomber completely unobserved, and blast away at the wing fuel tanks using incendiary rockets. The tanks would instantly catch on fire and explode. As a result a very small percentage of crews had time to bale out.

CHAPTER 9

OPERATIONS

I was now in charge of my own crew and given the awesome responsibility of taking them over enemy territory. Let me describe a typical Operation.

For a night flight the crew and I usually arrived at the briefing room at about 9 p.m. The Chief Navigation Officer uncovered a large wall map showing the target and the route to be followed to and from the target. He then asked for questions and handed over the floor to the Meteorological Officer, whose briefings we all took with a grain of salt because his predictions were usually far off the mark. When he predicted clear it could be solid overcast and we often experienced severe icing for part of the trip.

Next were the Bombing Officer, Intelligence Officer and Engineering Officer who each gave a briefing and answered questions pertaining to their respective departments.

Then it was time for the Commanding Officer, who always gave the same speech: "Well, chaps, I wish I could be going with you tonight. Unfortunately, that's not possible. However, the weather is going to be too bad over most of your route for Jerry night fighters to get off the ground, much less fly. You have been routed around most of the flak batteries. All in all this should be a piece of cake–nothing to it, chaps. Good luck! See you in the mess for breakfast!"

Last came the station Padre who said a prayer for our safe return.

Then it was off to our lockers to put on our flying gear and lock away our personal items.

By the time we were all geared up the crew bus would be waiting to take us out to the aircraft. There we would usually lie around on the ground nearby until boarding time.

Without a doubt this was the worst time for me and, I assume, for the rest of the crew who usually had very little to say. The nearer the time for take off the greater became my feelings of apprehension. I had to fight down my feelings as I climbed aboard and went through the checks, my mouth dry, my voice sounding high-pitched and unnatural.

You entered a Lancaster either through the main door behind the wings or up a ladder into the nose. When you reached the cockpit it seemed a long way from the ground. There was a long list of checks to go through before moving and several more before take off.

It wasn't easy to taxi along a winding track out to the runway. You turned by gunning the outer engine and straightened up by giving the opposite engine a burst, but there was a lot of inertia and you had to anticipate each turn. You had to keep a good grip on the brake lever otherwise the aircraft would get away from you.

The moments before take off were the most terrifying but once under way there was so much to do that it suddenly wasn't so bad. On take off you opened the throttle with your right hand, palm down, leading with the thumb on the port outer to counteract a tendency to swing left. You pushed the stick all the way forward to get the tail up as soon as possible, then you could steer with the rudders instead of the engines. With a full bomb load you stayed on the ground with the engineer calling out the speed. At 14O m.p.h. you pulled off the ground. On most occasions there was very little runway left.

After take off the Lancaster flew herself. She was undoubtedly a dream aircraft. By this time I always felt relaxed and confident.

The bombardier was down in the nose with the bomb sight and release gear. He could also man the front gun turret. One step up was the cockpit where I sat on the left and the flight engineer on the right on a fold-out seat. The bottom of my seat was reinforced with armour plating, the only place in the aircraft to be protected.

The navigator sat at a little desk behind me, facing left, with the wireless operator just aft of him. The navigator could take sextant shots of the stars through the astrodome above the wireless operator's right shoulder. Back down the fuselage aft of the cabin you passed a rest bed, used for emergencies, and came to the mid-upper gunner's turret sticking out of the roof. You squeezed past this to get to the Elsen toilet and finally to the rear gun turret poking out of the tail between the rudders.

With full fuel tanks and a normal bomb load the Lancaster climbed slowly. We were usually briefed to bomb from 20,000 feet but the last few hundred feet were hard to reach, especially on a warm night, so we had to climb the first 10,000 feet over base before setting course. The idea of hundreds of bombers circling together over a small area of Yorkshire was frightening, especially in clouds.

All of my crew were busy at this time and I was constantly checking them on the intercom: "Pilot to gunners–I just felt the slipstream of an aircraft. Keep a sharp

Lancaster in flight.

lookout." "Pilot to navigator–we are now approaching the coast. Have just levelled out at a cruising altitude of 18,000 feet. Please confirm our new heading is 042." "Pilot to bombardier–commence dumping window." "Window" was metal foil strips packaged in small bundles that were pushed through a special chute to break apart in the slipstream. This would confuse the German radar operators who instead of seeing a few aircraft on their screens would now see thousands of unidentified flying objects.

The flight engineer was kept busy monitoring the engine gauges and frequently transferring fuel from one tank to the next. Close attention had to be paid to the fuel consumption. He adjusted four mixture controls that would have to be pushed to full rich during evasive action then returned to lean for economical cruising as soon as possible afterwards.

The wireless operator kept a listening watch on his radio and from time to time would get a good radio bearing from an English station which he would immediately pass on to the navigator.

The navigator would take star shots with his sextant on clear nights in order to double check our position. From time to time he would instruct me to alter course on reaching a turning point, or he might tell me we were a little ahead or behind schedule. I then had to decrease or increase air speed in order to get back on schedule. On approach to the target he would advise that the P.F.F. would be marking the target in five minutes, at which time I would instruct the bombardier to report the markers going down. The bombardier would tell me to hold the aircraft absolutely level, with slight adjustments to left and right as he directed, until the bombs were away.

Every five to ten minutes I would call the gunners to make sure they were awake and alert. The rear gunner had the loneliest post on the aircraft, cut off from the rest of the crew except for the intercom. While the rest of the crew were kept warm by hot air ducts the rear gunner often had to endure temperatures of -50 degrees F.

There was constant noise in the aircraft. You could not hear anything that was going on outside, not even flak or other aircraft unless they were very close. You did hear whatever hit you and even rain and sleet sounded very loud. You could hear your own guns when they fired and feel how they made the aircraft throb. Over a hot target I always let my seat right down so I could concentrate on the bombing run without being put off by all the bright flashes.

Our targets were usually surrounded by flak and searchlight batteries and holding the aircraft steady was near impossible. It was like driving a fast speedboat into rough seas. Shortly after releasing our bombs we ran out of the flak batteries.

On my first command Op the middle upper gunner at this stage reported coloured tracers from a fighter. Seconds later we saw a mighty explosion followed by a large ball of fire heading towards the ground. I knew one of our bombers would not be returning. I silently prayed that the crew were able to bail out, but I doubted it. Fewer than five per cent of night bomber crews ever got out of a burning aircraft. This was a sobering experience and made us more alert than ever to the enemy night fighters that we knew were out there searching for us.

On landing back at base the crew bus would pick us up and take us to the Ops room for debriefing. Then it was off to the mess for bacon and eggs and back to our billets for sleep. Often I was so tense that I could not sleep. On these occasions I sometimes walked out to the aircraft parking area to see how many flak holes our mechanic had found in our fuselage and wings.

Not all Ops were routine, however. Just before my eighth Op on 27th April 1944 my brother Chester, now a Sub-lieutenant R.N.V.R. and in command of an L.C.T. ship, arrived to spend the night with me. We had planned a celebration for my recent promotion from Warrant Officer First Class to Flight Lieutenant, a jump of two ranks backdated six months–a nice little pay packet that I am sure my crew and Chester were anxious to help me spend.

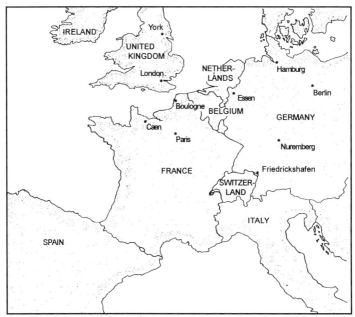

I was based at Linton-on-Ouse, which was located near York. I flew twenty-five bombing missions in Lancasters and Halifaxes to various destinations including Essen Nuremberg, Friedrichshafen, and Hamburg in Germany, and Boulogne, Caen, and other locations in occupied France.

Chester rode out to the aircraft with me and when I saw him climb into the front seat of the returning crew bus, driven by a pretty little W.A.A.F., I hoped he would not be too lonely while I was away. To this day he claims he spent the entire night in the control room, waiting for my return.

Our target was Friedrichshafen and we ran into intense flak. Thirty-six aircraft were lost on this mission. On the return journey, after completing our bombing, we ran into thunderstorms and a fierce headwind which caused heavy icing. As a result we ran low on fuel and I landed at Ford, an emergency airport in Ireland. By the time we refuelled and arrived back at base Chester was convinced he had seen the last of me.

On May 7th the reliable Lancaster was withdrawn from our squadron for some unknown reason and replaced by the Halifax Mark III. The changeover was definitely not welcome. The veterans in particular felt they stood a better chance of completing their tour of 30 Ops in the Lancaster.

Despite all the grumbling that the previous owners were anxious to get rid of the Halifax III, the conversions were quickly completed. There were some advantages. The Halifax was much faster and had further range, a greater service ceiling and more room for the crew. But with all those pluses I still preferred the Lancaster; from a pilot's point of view there was no comparison.

The navigator and wireless operator were now down in the nose almost under my feet in two cubicles. The navigator now had plenty of room to spread out his charts, The wireless operator had a new gadget to play with, an early radar system called H2S which provided very helpful information for the navigator. The bombardier sat or lay in a prone position on the escape hatch. In an emergency the hatch was easily jettisoned and provided our best means of leaving the aircraft. Directly behind my back was a bulkhead with a recess for my parachute. In this area the flight engineer sat with all the fuel controls and a duplicate set of engine instruments.

In an emergency, after I had given the order to bail out, the flight engineer was supposed to retrieve my parachute and pass it to me on his way out down a flight of six steps to the nose exit. It was a long way to the middle-upper gunner's turret and much further to the rear gunner's position.

Even though I had previously been checked out in an earlier model Halifax, I had to put in fifteen hours of training with my crew before my first Op in the Halifax Mark III over enemy territory.

Our first mission in the Halifax III was on 31st May to Au Fevre, France. We experienced gale force winds all along track, making it impossible for German fighters to fly.

Many of our targets at this time were in France, in preparation for and support of the D-Day invasion. On June 7th we bombed a V-2 rocket site at Acheres and on June 15th took part in our first daylight raid to Boulogne.

It was comforting to be able to see the crew for a change. There were no fiery red balls hurtling up from the ground, no frightening searchlights to blind you, no fighters to sneak up unseen under your aircraft's belly to blast you out of the sky. The exploding flak now left puffs of smoke like small mushroom clouds that would still rock the aircraft when they exploded nearby. It was easier by daylight to avoid the flak batteries grouped together around a radar station because you could see any concentrations of flak bursts from a long way off.

The biggest problem of daylight missions was flying in formation. We were not as experienced as our American allies in this type of flying and we were hard pressed to stay in orderly formation. In my opinion there was no comparison with night bombing. As the English often said, "Daytime bombing is a piece of cake!"

Everyone welcomed these 'milk runs' because they counted towards a tour completion of 30 Ops just as the longer trips at night did. In reality, however, there was no such thing as a milk run. Every mission was fraught with danger and the first flight over enemy territory was often the last for many good crews.

On July 5th we flew in support of Canadian forces approaching Caen. Our targets were German tanks, artillery and fortifications around the city. The Army commander was very pleased with the results and sent a message of thanks to our command. It had been a wonderfully impressive show which was enormously appreciated by the Army–so much so that we repeated the performance at Biennais two days later.

CHAPTER 10

THE FINAL OPERATION

Within the short period of nine months I had successfully completed 24 Ops bombing enemy targets. In the meantime we put in many hours practice bombing targets in several sites around England, and other related crew-training programmes.

Occasionally my crew would join my friend, Harry Facey, and his crew. We would all take our bikes for a ride around the beautiful English countryside, stopping at our favourite pub for a pint of beer and a game or two of darts.

Once a month we were given a 48-hour pass. As a rule we all headed to London. My first stop there was the West Indies Committee Building to check for mail and news from home, and hopefully to meet one of my friends for a weekend of fun and games. But my most memorable weekend was with a gentleman farmer, Mr. Markham, and his wife.

The Markhams had befriended my brother Chester and shortly thereafter I received a letter from them inviting my crew and me for a weekend at the farm. Enclosed with the invitation was a detailed map of the area showing their farm in relation to the town of Ely.

It so happened there was a practice bombing range not too far away so I decided that on my next training mission I would drop a note from our aircraft down to the Markham farm. My crew was enthusiastic when I told them of my plans and they all joined me in preparing our grateful acceptance of the kind invitation.

The note of thanks and acceptance was wrapped in a tiny package and a long multi-coloured cloth tail was attached. In the note we also asked the Markhams to wave a white cloth when they found the package.

A few days later I convinced my Flight Commander that my crew needed additional bombing practice. He readily agreed and praised my crew and me for being so dedicated.

It was a beautiful clear day when we flew over Ely on our way to the practice range and I had no trouble spotting the Markham's farm. After our assignment at the practice range was completed I flew back to the Markham's farm and circled at a very low altitude. In no time, three people appeared on the large front lawn. We went down to about 100 feet for our "bombing" run. On my final circle we were pleased to see them all frantically waving large white cloths. We knew our 'bomb' had landed on target. I later found out that Mr. Markham had caught the cloth tail before it settled to the ground.

On our next 48-hour pass we all headed for the farm. What a grand time we had! We were overfed and entertained and introduced to many of the neighbours. They were all wonderful, friendly people who reminded me so much of the western Canadian farmers. It brought home to me that I could not judge the English by a few of their overbearing officers.

A few years after the war was over, Mrs. Markham came to Nassau as the house guest of Chester. We were all overjoyed to see her and glad of the opportunity to try and repay the kindness we had received from those English farmers so long ago.

In spite of the pressures of war, I was walking on lighter feet these days. Whatever my success in the major theatre, I had accomplished my mission back home. Mary was pregnant and, if I survived, I would become a father.

On 28th July 1944 we took off at 2230 hours in a Halifax to bomb one of the industrial areas on the outskirts of Hamburg. We had a bomb load of sixteen 500 lb. bombs and ten cans of incendiary bombs.

In addition to my regular crew we had on board P/O Heron for his first indoctrination flight with a veteran pilot.

He introduced himself to the crew and said, "All my friends call me Jinx." How true that turned out to be.

Right from the start I had trouble. First the port outboard engine was slow in starting. When we finally got it started we discovered a bad magneto drop. I talked it over with my flight engineer and we decided it might clear up once we were airborne. The delay caused me to lose my turn for take off and I was the last to go.

On rolling onto the runway I failed to go forward far enough to straighten my tail and lock it. When I opened the throttles fully and released the brakes, the aircraft swerved to port off the runway and onto the grass. It took me a while to get it back onto the runway. Because of these manoeuvres I had used up some precious take off distance and I had to pull back on the control column at the last moment, barely missing the trees at the end of the runway. We had finished our slow turn over the aerodrome before I managed to relax.

We crossed the French coast at 20,000 feet and soon ran into dark towering clouds, heavy rain, icing and lightning. The lightning was so bright I had to break regulations and turn on the cockpit lights to the maximum so I was not blinded.

To make matters worse my air speed indicator started acting up and then quit. I guessed the pitot tube had iced up but there was nothing I could do. Under normal circumstances the A.S.I. is necessary in order not to get into a stall, which could easily happen when you do not know your air speed. I considered putting the nose down and returning to base, but the thought of ploughing into another aircraft and my own stupid pride kept me from doing so. The one comforting thought was that it was too bad for the Luftwaffe night fighters to be flying.

Twenty minutes from our target we ran out of the clouds into a beautiful clear star-filled sky. There was a heavy concentration of flak all around the city of Hamburg, fiery red bursts no doubt brought on by the first wave of bombers which was two minutes ahead of us. There were three waves of bombers that night, each wave comprising 100 bombers.

Right on time the marker flares went down directly in front of us followed by the welcome voice through our headphones: "Hello, main bomber force, this is Black Tie One. Aim your bombs at the centre of the red and green markers."

I made my run following the instructions of Bombardier Cuff: "Steady, steady...Right, right... Hold it... Bombs away... Close doors." A minute later the navigator called: "Commence your turn now to a new heading of - "

A tremendous explosion occurred just behind my seat in the flight engineer's compartment. The controls were wrenched out of my hands. Another explosion followed a little further aft. The aircraft became an instant inferno.

The following is from the history of 426 Squadron:

Hamburg too was heavily defended by flak batteries when 16 Thunderbird Halifaxes raided the city on the 28th. One large orange red explosion was seen in the target area, and the crews believed it was probably a good show. But two good crews went missing. The captains were F/Lt. L. M. Thompson and F/S P.B. Eagles. There were no survivors from the second crew but the pilot, second pilot F/O Heron and wireless operator F/O G.H. Fewetrall in F/Lt. Thompson's crew were taken prisoner. Some equipment in his Halifax went unserviceable on the outward journey but Thompson continued to the target, released his bombs and started for home. Then, according to his report, "Suddenly out of the blue a terrific explosion occurred around the engineer's position followed instantly by a second explosion. With the explosion came fire, from the port inner engine to the fuselage and inside the bomb bay from engineer's position to rest position. Ordered crew to bale out. Put George the automatic pilot in control and then proceeded to get out myself. I had 'chute on and my hand on the release ready to dive through the escape hatch. The next thing I remember is waking up wondering why it was so deathly quiet. Before I had fully recovered my senses, my 'chute caught in a tree and I came to rest a few feet off the deck." F/O Heron, who was captured after evading for two days, thought the attack might have been made by incendiary rockets fired from the vertical guns of a fighter. Fewetrall was injured in the attack and spent six months in a German hospital recuperating.

For what seemed like a very long time I hung like a spider on a thread from a tall tree. The night was pitch black and I could not see the ground. I could hear sirens wailing in the distance and dogs barking nearby. I heard a clank, clank noise that grew louder by the second, then a train passed by some 40 or 50 feet up a steep embankment from where I hung trapped in my parachute harness.

Had the harness fitted properly the release lock would have been positioned in the middle of my chest and one good bang with my hand would have freed me. As it was, my harness had been made for someone much taller than me and the release lock was way above my head. When I finally worked free I only dropped about five or six feet before hitting the ground.

Barking dogs were getting closer. I quickly scrambled up the embankment and when I hit the railroad track I started running in the opposite direction. It was then 2 a.m. and we had released our bombs at 1:31 a.m.

I ran and walked along the track until I came to a small railway station near a village. I left the track and made a detour around the village. Much later another railway station loomed up and I could hear the clank of an approaching train. Day was breaking and it was getting light so I left the track again to find shelter in the nearby woodland.

Airmen were issued with full instructions as to what to do once stranded in enemy territory. It was felt we would be in a state of shock and would not be thinking very clearly so there were knock-out pills in our escape kits that would put us to sleep for about twelve hours. After that we should be able to think clearly.

I had no sooner entered the woods when I became violently sick, so much so that I could not stand. I lay on the ground too sick to move out of my own vomit. When I finally stood I realised I was barefoot, my feet a mess of cuts and bruises. Apparently my suede fleece-lined flying boots had blown off some time after I had jumped from the aircraft. It was into my roomy boots that I had stuffed my escape kit–chocolate bars, food bars, European currency, maps, compass, flashlight and pills. All were lost.

My face and head felt very painful. I discovered leaves and soil sticking to open blisters on my face. My eyebrows and hair were burned off. I realised I had been burned when I went to retrieve my parachute from its stowage in the bulkhead directly behind my seat in the engineer's compartment where the first explosion had occurred.

All morning I lay in the woods in a position where I could watch the railway station. On two occasions a train pulled in and people got off and headed to the little village on the far side of the track.

I noticed that after every train departure a man in uniform would pass quite close to my hiding place and disappear down a track into the woods. By cautiously moving in the same direction I discovered a small house on the edge of the trees.

Next time the uniformed man came out of the house, closed the door and headed back to the station I made my move. All I wanted to do was clean up my face, get a bite to eat and maybe find a pair of shoes or something to wrap around my feet. I entered a fairly large room that appeared to be the kitchen and dining area. On the far wall were two doors that I assumed led to bedrooms.

I had just started to have a good look-around when one of the doors opened and in walked a middle-aged woman. She took one look at me and let out a scream that I am sure could have been heard a mile away: "Terror flieger! Luft gangster!"

In moments the man from the railway station came rushing in screaming the same words. He grabbed my arm

and started pulling me towards the door. The woman, obviously his wife, started railing at him in German and he promptly turned me loose. She was crying and went back into her room. The man and I just stood there.

The woman returned with a basin of water and motioned for me to sit while she cleaned my face, all the while arguing with her husband who was obviously anxious to get me out of the house. He kept looking towards the station.

When my face was clean and dry she gave me a drink that damned near choked me. I assumed it was high-proof schnapps. Only then, with tears in her eyes, did she let me go. She reminded me so much of my mother.

Many years after the war was over I went back with my wife, daughter and German son-in-law, who lived in Hamburg, and found the lady and her husband. They were retired and lived in a village near the railway station. They immediately recognised me and through my two interpreters (for my daughter spoke fluent German) we found out why she had been in tears that day. She had recently heard that her son, a Luftwaffe pilot, had been killed in action in Italy. I remained in contact with them until my daughter moved away from Hamburg several years later.

But I didn't know all about that at the time. All I knew was that I was a prisoner.

CHAPTER 11

CAPTURED!

My captor proved to be the railway station master. He led me over to the station and made a telephone call during which he referred to me as "American Luftgangster" and "Terrorfluger" several times. He was obviously reporting my capture and I prayed he was not talking to the Gestapo.

Word of my capture must have reached the little village near the station because the platform was soon filled with men, women and children. Some were quite aggressive and cursed and spat on me.

A big fat man broke through the crowd, took me by the arm and led me off a short distance. The first thing he said, in broken English, was, "For you *der var ist ofer*"–a phrase I was to hear over and over again during my P.O.W. days. "Where are you from in America?" he went on. "I lived in New York for ten years. Quick, give me your escape kit."

"I don't have it," I told him.

"Then tell me where you hid it," he insisted.

I was saved by the arrival of a train pulling two carriages. Two elderly uniformed men emerged pushing a bicycle and carrying ancient shotguns. A heated argument took place between the station master and the two new arrivals. It became obvious that the station master wanted them to sign a receipt for one sick, scared Abaco boy.

When this transaction was finally completed we started walking, with me pushing the bicycle. One German walked in front while the other walked behind with his gun pointed at my back. Out of the corner of my eye I could see the old lady who had tended me wiping away tears with her apron.

We walked for about an hour or more until we reached a small town. I was taken straight to the burgermeister's office. A uniformed man and a young girl arrived and the man's first words were: "For you *der var ist ofer!*"

The young girl spoke fluent English and asked me many questions. All she learned from me was my name and rank. I was searched but all they found was a watch, a comb and a photo of Mary. These were taken from me and placed in an envelope. I was issued a receipt for them.

All night long I sat on a hard wooden bench with my elderly guards watching me, guns at hand.

Early next morning a Luftwaffe major arrived and, in perfect English, told me he was from the Luftwaffe station in Lubeck and asked me to accompany him. Outside was parked a large chauffeur-driven car. The chauffeur saluted and opened the rear door for me. The major followed me in and the chauffeur closed the door.

"I'm so glad I was able to get you before the Gestapo arrived," the major told me. "You are now in the hands of the Luftwaffe. We fliers must stick together. Not all Germans are like the Gestapo." He chatted pleasantly, mainly aeroplane talk, but I sensed he was very cleverly trying to extract information from me such as the type of aircraft I had been flying, the name of my squadron leader, and any special equipment I had on board.

At the entrance to the Lubeck aerodrome the major handed me over to the guards. He shook my hand and wished me well. "I will see what can be done about your face and a pair of boots," he said as he left. I never saw him again.

The building I was escorted into was a typical guard house like those found on any airfield in Canada or England. A corridor led off the guard room with four cells on each side. I was pushed inside one and the door was closed with a bang.

The cell measured eight feet by ten and had one small barred window. Instead of a bed there was a mound of straw in a corner. The overhead light was controlled from outside and now and then it would be switched on and a face would appear in the peep hole in the door. A short length of rope hung just inside the door. When this was pulled, a wooden arm on the outside fell with a bang. This was the signal for the guard to escort me to the *abort* or toilet.

I spent a wretched night in the cell. Sleep was impossible because my face was hurting and the straw was full of fleas.

In the late morning W/O Fewetrall was brought in and placed in the cell opposite. During the afternoon I was given three slices of bread and some water.

The following afternoon P/O Heron was brought in and led to a cell down the corridor, too far away to let him know where I was. It was good to know I was not the only survivor.

Right from the beginning of my captivity I kept a diary which I have to this day. The entries are not all grammatically correct nor do they keep to strict tense structure. They do, however, capture the essence of what happened to me better than a later transcription:

> July 31st - Left the prison at Lubeck during early morning. Heron and Fewetrall with me, also three armed guards. Destination unknown. Train very crowded. We have been heading in a westerly direction since starting. The countryside is very beautiful.
>
> 1800 hours - Arrived at the Interrogation Centre Dulag Luft, 30 miles N.E. Frankfort. After a minor interrogation escorted to a small cell. The other prison cell was like a palace compared to this torture chamber. The room is 8 feet long and 5 feet wide with a low ceiling. At the end is one small window that has been painted over. Below the window taking up the full width of the room is a large heater. One overhead light. One metal cot with a lumpy burlap sack filled with straw. Light and heater controlled from outside in corridor. Tem-

perature of cell almost unbearable when heater on. The metal on the bed gets so hot I fear the straw mattress might catch fire. Placed it on floor as far away as possible from the heater. When heater is off the room is still like a sauna as the thick concrete walls and floor retain the heat. The place is teeming with body lice.

August 1st - The interrogation began very early when I was escorted into a large office where a high ranking officer sat behind a desk and pretended to be a Swiss Red Cross representative. I was told to sit then handed a lengthy form to fill out and told that immediately on completing the form my family and squadron would be notified that I was alive and well.

The form started innocently enough by asking for name, rank and number which, according to the Geneva Convention, was all we were required to give. Following this was name of squadron leader, address of next of kin, what special equipment was being carried in aircraft, name of commanding officer and on and on for twenty or more questions. I filled in the first three and then the name and address of Mary. I handed the paper back unsigned explaining that it was against our regulations for me to complete the form.

The interrogator put on a sad, pained expression and said, "I only wanted to let your family and squadron know you are safe. How else can we prove that you are indeed a pilot and not a spy or a saboteur. I might believe you but I seriously doubt if the Gestapo will, and that's who you will be turned over to if you do not cooperate. I suggest you spend a few days in your cell and think about this."

August 2nd - In my cell all day, no food or water, the heater going full blast, the heat is unbearable. After repeated requests I was allowed to take my slop bucket and empty the contents in a toilet down the hall. What a relief to get out of the cell for even a few moments. Back in my cell I stand and sit, looking forward to my next interrogation which will take me out for a while.

August 3rd - Interrogated by Lt. Schum who spoke with an English accent. He had lived in England and the U.S.A. for many years before the war. The interrogation started off in a very friendly manner by him offering me a cigarette, which I declined, then a chocolate bar that I gladly accepted. Then came the form that I had previously refused to complete. I refused to take it from him.

The friendly approach suddenly changed. He started shouting, threatening to have me shot. He passed me cutouts from U.S. and Canadian newspapers. "Read these," he said. "See how many Jews have made millions out of the war making uniforms for young stupid boys."

The news clippings were all about the millions that were being made in various war-related industries by large companies. I saw no mention of Jews. When I drew this to his attention he hit the ceiling again and continued to rant about how the Jews had destroyed Germany after World War I. He finally calmed down and said, "I don't understand how a young Bahamian like you would come over here and bomb innocent women and children. What have we Germans done to you?"

August 4th - I am very discouraged, hungry, and can't sleep for the heat and lice.

August 5th - Interrogated again. What a relief to get out of the heat. I complained bitterly about the way I was treated, comparing my treatment with German prisoners in Canada who were well fed and treated with respect and consideration.

August 6th - In my sauna cell all day. 3 slices of bread and a small cup of potato soup late in the evening. My face very painful.

August 7th - Interrogated again with the usual threats about turning me over to the Gestapo. At the end I was told by Lt. Schum that I would be leaving in the morning. My watch, comb and Mary's picture were returned to me. I was escorted to another room where I was fingerprinted and photographed.

August 8th - 0700 hours, guard arrived and took me to a large room filled with American uniforms and shoes. I was left alone in the room and told to find a pair of shoes. I picked a pair one size too large as my feet were swollen and too sore to get them on. I was then escorted to a large waiting room and was surprised to find the room packed with U.S. Air Force crew members and a few Canadians and Australians.

No one spoke. There was absolute quiet. I approached one of the Canadians and he promptly put his finger to his lips and pointed towards the ceiling. Obviously the room was bugged.

After sitting around for a couple of hours we were taken out and told we would be moving to Dulag Luft, about 40 miles away. What a shock when we arrived at this camp! We were met at the gate by Col. Sark of the U.S. who told us this was a transit camp run by the Swiss Red Cross. He and other prisoners, including doctors, had volunteered their services.

Luftwaffe military kept a close watch and patrolled the high barbed wire fence that completely enclosed the camp.

We were taken to the showers where we cleaned and deloused ourselves and our clothes. Then on to the stores. First came a small cardboard suitcase, toilet articles, change of underwear, socks, shirt and a diary. *(I still have the diary and have referred to it extensively as a reminder of dates, places and unfolding events during my P.O.W. life.)*

We then went to the mess hall for a great meal, then off to the doctor where my face was properly cleaned and treated with a black tarry ointment.

I now feel better than I have since that fateful night so long ago. Wrote a card to Mary and got a promise from the Red Cross that they would immediately notify my squadron of my whereabouts.

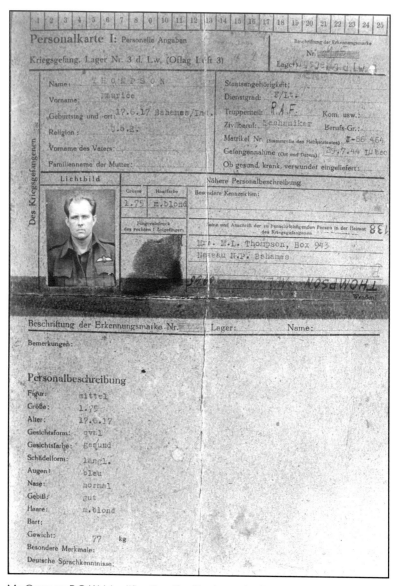

My German P.O.W. identification. The Russians who liberated Stalag Luft III forwarded this identification to the Swiss Red Cross who eventually mailed it to me in Nassau.

August 10th - 0800 hours, told we are moving to Stalag Luft III near Sagan, Belaria. 1730, escorted to railway station. Travelling in an old Italian carriage with wooden seats, 10 men to a compartment with seats for only 6 men. Very uncomfortable night. Took turns standing.

August 11th - All day on the train. No food.

August 12th - 1400 hours, arrived at Sagan. American airmen staying here. Told that the rest of us will be moving on to another compound.

CHAPTER 12

STALAG LUFT III

As we approached the gate there were about a hundred airmen lined up just inside the warning wire waiting to meet the new "purge"–the word used to describe the transfer of P.O.W.s I heard a familiar voice calling: "Bahamas! Bahamas! What took you so long? I've been expecting you." It was my old friend Harry Facey, who had gone missing a few months earlier.

Before entering the camp we were escorted to the guard house where we were photographed, fingerprinted and body-searched, a humiliating and pointless procedure to me. Then we entered Stalag Luft III North Camp, situated near the town of Sagan some 90 miles south-east of Berlin.

Harry Facey greeted me when I entered and told me that as I had been positively identified I could proceed directly to Building 104 Room 17. This screening was necessary in order to expose German spies dressed as airmen who frequently came through with a new purge of P.O.W.s. One of the spies had committed suicide recently and the Germans would be more careful in the future.

The North Compound was a square about 350 yards on each side. In the northern half of the compound were long barracks, called blocks. Each block had three rows of five buildings. There was a man-made fire pool that held water to extinguish fires, a kitchen, and three or four large latrine buildings. These were built over deep pits and inside each was an island-style 12-hole toilet that provided a great place to hear all the rumours. Fastened onto the walls were long urinals of bent tin which drained towards corner pipes.

The southern half of the compound had been cleared

as an exercise area which was also used for our twice-daily roll calls. The whole camp was enclosed by double barbed wire fences standing ten feet high and five feet apart, with coils of concertina wire on the ground between them. Inside the main fence was a 40 foot wide strip of sand, marked by a three foot high warning rail. The guards would automatically shoot anyone who put his foot on the warning rail or stepped onto the sand.

Outside the northern wire was the *Vorlager* which housed the German guard room, the hospital, and the cooler for solitary confinement. The *Vorlager* had two gates, one leading to the compound itself and the other to the main dirt road outside. Every two or three hundred feet around the compound were elevated guard towers (we called them "goon boxes"). Inside each box was a sentry equipped with search lights and automatic weapons. At night more sentries patrolled outside. Inside the fence a *hundfuhrer* patrolled with a German shepherd or Doberman pinscher, trained to attack on command and go for the throat. The German name for us was "kriegies"–prisoners.

The camp population was predominantly British, which then meant English, Canadian, Welsh, Scottish, Northern Irish, New Zealanders, Australians, South Africans, Trinidadians and, of course, a Bahamian. But other countries were well represented, including Chile, Malaya, Mauritius, Norway, Poland, Holland, Belgium and Denmark.

When I first arrived we had adequate room facilities but the blocks began to fill up quickly as the weeks went by. A block was divided into 16 or 18 rooms with two more rooms large enough for two men at the end of the building. These were reserved for the senior officers. One corner room held the night latrine with indoor plumbing.

When I first arrived, each of the larger rooms had six double bunk beds, a small kitchen table and four chairs. Each bunk was lined with hard bedboards topped with a thin mattress stuffed with straw, which looked like a long burlap sack. Every block had a communal wash room in which we could shave and wash our hands and face.

The kitchen held a small coal stove and tiny oven

Drawn by a Polish POW at Stalag Luft III in exchange for a cigarette, this sketch shows me at the camp with a "goon box" in the background.

and was certainly not designed to feed a hundred men. The mess was organised into shifts so everyone could get a time to cook and eat. The one large kitchen building outside the blocks was used primarily to provide hot water in large quantities for tea and coffee, when available. Two or three times a week our kriegie staff, consisting of non-commissioned airmen, would cook a thin barley or cabbage soup with a few potatoes when we could get them from the Germans.

The German bread was usually so mouldy we had to toast it before eating. What really sustained us were the Red Cross parcels sent in via Switzerland from countries such as the U.S., Canada, Australia, New Zealand and Britain. Canned powdered milk was always included in the American parcels and the tins were almost as valuable as the contents–klim, milk spelt backwards. The taste brought back memories of the drink I had enjoyed many times from my grandmother in Hope Town, which now seemed so very far away. The Klim cans were used for cooking pots and many other things–including escape tools.

The cooking was done on a rotation basis. We had a room roster that showed when each person was to cook. Each cook had helper, or "stooge" as we called him, who would do the mundane jobs such as peel potatoes and clean up. All the food from Red Cross parcels and German rations would go into a common pool that would be carefully hoarded and watched over. It would be apportioned just before cooking time and the cook would have to be very careful to be fair–or else!

Cigarettes and chocolate bars included in Red Cross parcels were not pooled but went to the recipients. They were traded like gold and, being a non-smoker, I was able to barter for items I desperately needed such as warm wool socks. Sometimes, when food was short and people were getting hungry, a candy bar would be traded for the equivalent of twenty dollars.

When not thinking and talking about food, there were a number of other activities to fill the long and restless hours. Some of the older prisoners who had been receiving parcels for years would be generous in sharing books, games and playing cards with the new kriegies. It was always easy to find partners for any activity.

When the weather was good we would stroll around the camp on what we would call "a circuit." On my second or third day in the camp I went on a circuit with Harry Facey. We stopped for a while chatting with a friend of Harry's. Without thinking, the friend casually put his foot on the warning wire to tie his shoelace. There was an instant crack of a rifle, followed by blood all over the place.

"My God, the Nazi bastard has shot my hand off!" Harry's friend screamed. Sure enough, his hand was hanging by a string. We rushed him to the hospital where his hand was amputated. This was a frightening experience. It brought home to me that some of the guards were cruel, heartless bastards.

I spent a lot of time trying to sleep and, as it got colder and our food rations dwindled, I spent more and more time resting and trying to stay warm.

At least twice a day all activities were interrupted for a roll call. The first was in the morning between six and eight o'clock. The guards would walk through the block stepping into each room and yelling, "Rouse - Rouse, schnell!"

We would all head for the parade grounds and, on order, line into five ranks behind our barracks commander. This made it easy for the Germans to count us and know who was responsible for an absence. The second roll call, or *appell,* was late in the afternoon. If an escape was suspected we would be called out in the middle of the night or any time they felt like it. Unfortunately, these night rouses would sometimes turn riotous when some smart-assed airman decided to jump ranks or hide behind one of the blocks. The rest would be forced to stand at attention while the barracks were thoroughly searched.

Many of the older prisoners were involved in escape plans. Just before my arrival some eighty airmen had escaped through a tunnel from one of the barracks. Fifty of the officers were caught and shot by the Gestapo on 27th March 1944. Only three of the remainder made it safely back to England. The rest were caught and returned to camp where they spent weeks in solitary confinement. Many years later a movie was made about the venture: "The Great Escape," starring the late Steve McQueen. I learned a lot about that famous attempt at freedom.

The entrance to the tunnels was well camouflaged and went down thirty feet before turning towards the woods. It ran for 300 feet underground, passing the goon boxes, and was supposed to break out near the woods. Unfortunately, this was not the case.

The first airman out of the hole discovered, to his horror, that he was much nearer the goon boxes than the woods. The hole was also in the direct path of the patrolling guard. This slowed the operation down. Even so, eighty men surfaced and slithered on their bellies into the woods. Finally, with daylight approaching, a guard spotted the exit hole and raised the alarm.

Those tunnels were a great feat of engineering under the circumstances. One of the main architects was Wally Floody, a Canadian engineer who had worked in the mines before joining the R.C.A.F. Three tunnels were under construction for several years. They were named Tom, Dick and Harry in order to disguise what they really were in regular conversation.

During my confinement, a top secret senior group known as the X Organisation was responsible for escapes and security. They supervised such covert activities as transmitting radio messages to the Allies and hiding forbidden items such as cameras and printing equipment. Most of this equipment was obtained, ironically, from German guards who were skillfully compromised then blackmailed into collaboration.

Our living quarters were constantly searched. We referred to the specially-trained Germans who pried as "Ferrets." They spoke fluent English and sneaked around with long screwdrivers which they used to probe the ground, looking for a tunnel. A very effective system of internal stooges and listening posts kept track of their movements whenever they entered the camp.

At the gate, a kriege called the Duty Pilot would follow each Ferret. Word got through to controllers who would analyse the Ferrets' activities from how many there were, what time of day it was, and where they were headed. If they got too close to a tunnel under construction or some other clandestine activity, a signal was sent and a diversion set up. I sometimes volunteered as Duty Pilot.

Not all prisoners wanted to escape, I should explain. The recent arrivals were more aware that the war was approaching its end and knew, even if we escaped, we would be unable to contribute any further. Those who had experienced years of incarceration were more impatient. But all prisoners were willing to assist in escape plans.

The following is a poem from my P.O.W. diary written in the cooler one day in April 1943 by F/Lt. E. Gordon Brettell after one of his early attempts to escape:

If you can quit the compound undetected
And clear your tracks, nor leave the slightest trace,
And follow out the programme you've selected
Nor lose your grasp of distance, time and space -

If you can walk at night by compass bearing
Or ride the rails in light of day,
And temper your elusiveness with daring,
Trusting that sometimes bluff will find a way -

If you can swallow sudden sour frustration
And gaze unmoved on failure's ugly shape,
Remembering as further inspiration
It was and is your duty to escape -

If you can keep the great Gestapo guessing
With explanations only partly true,
And leave them in their heart of hearts confessing
They didn't get the whole truth out of you -

If you can use your cooler fortnight clearly
For planning methods wiser than before,

And treat your first miscalculations merely
As hints let fall by fate to teach you more -

If you scheme on with patience and precision
(It wasn't in a day they builded Rome)
And make escape your single sole ambition -
The next time you attempt you will get home!

Gordon Brettell was shot to death with forty-nine other officers on March 27th 1944 after escaping from Sagan for the fourth time.

Time went by and colder weather arrived, making it near impossible to spend any time outside. To make matters worse, our Red Cross parcels were reduced to half a parcel per man per week. Soon they were cut altogether. The German rations consisted of two potatoes and three slices of bread a day. Once or twice a week we would get a bowl of potato, beet or kohlrabi soup. To this day I cannot abide kohlrabi. Occasionally we would receive margarine or jam with our bread ration. This jam was made from ground-up sugar beet and served as a poor excuse for marmalade.

Something the Germans really liked and I could not stand was "fischkase" (fish cheese). I don't know how it was made; I do know for certain that it smelled of dead fish. To eat it, I had to close my eyes and hold my nose.

The twice-daily trips outside to be counted became miserable chores that nobody looked forward to once the cold weather set in. Most of us huddled down in bed trying to keep warm, even using German propaganda newspapers to cover up with. The most trivial incident with a roommate would blow up into a shouting match, then curses and raised fists.

Some of the contention gravitated around the English. Many of them hated the "Yanks" and constantly spewed out diatribes against the Americans. The Colonials, including one lone Bahamian, defended the Americans. "You're jealous of them fighting for and winning their independence," I would tell the English.

Back to my diary.

October 11th 1944 - Every day seems colder than the day before. Such long, dreary days dreaming of home and my favourite dishes. In my more depressed moments I lie in my sack and wonder why I should suffer while so many healthy so-called men are roaming around at home with no barbed wire,–plenty of food,–money piling up in the bank and a secure future that many of us have suffered and died for.

October 20th - With the exception of a few tough Canadians who still go outside to skate on the fire pool that has been frozen over for the past few weeks, the rest of us only venture outside when it is absolutely necessary.

December 12th - Received my first letter from Mary today. Was cheered up so much I went outside and walked around the circuit. Am now determined to survive no matter what the Germans do to me or how tough the going gets.

The arrival of the mail was an exciting time for us, especially to those who received a letter from home. The letters were usually passed around. Sometimes a "Dear John" arrived and the recipient would be so mad he would post it on the bulletin board.

My favourite letter of this ilk was from the fiancee of an airman:

Darling,

You have been gone so long that I have married your father.

Love,
Mother.

More mischievous was a letter from someone called Colin to one of my fellow P.O.W.s.

Dear Robert,

Nothing doing over here in Toronto, but I sure do envy you being over there fighting those Jerries. I was over to see your wife Mabel the other night. She lets me read all your letters. They're a bit mushy but I don't blame you, Robert. She's sure some sexy broad. And what a figure! The guys just stand and stare when she walks down the street. I guess you don't know that Patrick is rooming at your place. He says it is convenient as it is so close to work and saves him a lot of gas and meals.

Well, Robert, it's getting late so I will close. I can see your house from here and am watching Mabel and Patrick through the windows. He's wearing your red pyjamas and they are having a nightcap.

Well, Robert, I wish I could be over there with you. Give those Jerries hell.

Your friend,
Colin.

PS - If you hear any rumour that Mabel is pregnant, pay no attention to it. It all started when she forgot to pay the water bill and someone overheard her tell Patrick she was overdue.

We all laughed outwardly at these cruel letters but they gnawed inwardly. None of us were old enough to have a secure relationship. Our world was terribly confined and the outside world was seen through barbed wire fence. Our homes seemed a million miles away.

CHAPTER 13

FREEDOM

December 25th 1944 - Christmas here at last and what a lot of sick kriegies! Late yesterday the Germans gave each man one half of a Red Cross parcel. We had one big bash with no thought of tomorrow. It's fairly warm for a change. Most of my roommates were up early and out for a walk.

January 21st 1945 - Last night's news was very good. The Russians are reported to be making great advances in our direction.

January 22nd - All day long German refugees have been streaming by our camp, most of them in horse-drawn carts or sleighs piled high with boxes, bedding, little children and old women. It must be hell for those children. The German guards are getting very friendly. They are scared to death of the Russians and they have every reason to be. They treat the Russians like animals. They are used around the camp mainly for cleaning out the refuse from our outside toilets, which is then pumped into large wooden tanks and taken to the fields to be used as fertilizer. They are poorly dressed, many of them with rags tied around their feet for shoes. It's easy to believe rumours that thousands of them have died since the cold set in.

January 23rd - If possible, it's much colder today. The fields are covered in snow and the roads are solid ice. The refugees are still going by. Also thousands of German Army recruits, mostly old men and young boys–all on foot. The Russians are getting nearer. We can now hear their artillery banging away.

January 25 - Still the refugees stream by in ever
greater numbers. General opinion in the camp is that the Germans will try to evacuate us. A small minority believe we will be executed before the Russians arrive and we should be ready to make a break for the Russian lines. With the small amount of food we have been getting for the past few months and the generally low physical state that prevails throughout the camp, any long march or escape attempt in this weather would be deadly. Few of us would survive. I am down to 125 lbs. I have lost 40 lbs. since July 28th, the night I was shot down.

January 26th - Refugees still going by. The Russians are getting very close. We can hear small arms explosions. 21 U.S. Non-Commissioned Officers out of 1500 arrived here today. They were force-marched and reported that when they dropped and could not walk they were shot and left on the road. The condition of these survivors is beyond description. They marched 120 Km. from a P.O.W. camp near Breslau.

January 27th - It's bitterly cold. The water in our room freezes up.

22.00 hours - Ordered by the guards to be ready to move in 20 minutes. The Germans are in a panic and utter confusion prevails throughout the camp. After waiting around for several hours, allowed back to our rooms. Three of my friends–Cy, Alf and Ray–and I have built a rough sled from bed boards and part of a Red Cross box. Should come in handy for the forced march. Spent a sleepless night waiting for the word to move.

January 28th - Word came just after daylight. We quickly assembled outside, 40 or 50 men in a column with one guard at the head of the column, the other at the rear. Both were well-armed and had a German shepherd on a leash. Just before moving off we were given half of a Red Cross food parcel each. These, along with our personal effects, were loaded onto our sled.

Just before dark we took over a barn in a farmyard where we spent a wretched night. Pushing the sled was not too bad and Klim mixed with snow gave us some energy. Without it, many of us would not have survived. We walked 21 Km. today. Even the guards do not know where we are going. It seems that the main object is to stay ahead of the Russians.

January 29th - Commenced walking again at 06.00 hours. Not so cold today. We only covered 17 Km. when we marched into a big farmyard and found good beds in the loft of a barn with plenty of good, dry, clean hay. Fell asleep immediately.

January 30th - Told we are not moving today. Given one cup of barley soup by the farmer. Gave a Polish farmhand two cigarettes to dry my socks and shoes.

Drawn in my POW diary by a friend to commemorate our forced march from Sagan-Balaria to Lukenwald in January 1945.

January 31st - 08.00 hours, on the move again. We take turns pushing and pulling the sled.

February 1st - Not moving today.

February 2nd - Much warmer today. Most of the snow and ice melted during the night. Today's walk was the toughest going yet. Had to abandon our sled. Just after dark we were herded into another barn. Polish prisoners on the farm traded us cooked potatoes for cigarettes. Walked 25 Km. today.

February 3rd - Commenced walking early. After a few hours arrived at the town of Spremburg where we were given a small ration of soup and one slice of bread. Later we were marched to the railway station where we boarded a cattle wagon - standing room only. Rumour has it we are going to a P.O.W. camp somewhere near Berlin.

February 4th - Arrived at Lukenwald railway station then walked 6 Km. to the prison camp. On entering, searched by an English-speaking German then escorted to our compound where I was assigned a cot in a barracks building for Air Force officers. Never in my wildest dreams would I believe that a human being would have to live in such a crowded, filthy hole. I soon discovered that the dirty bed was infested with body lice. I was so tired that, in spite of it all, when I hit the bed I fell asleep immediately.

February 5th - Terribly tired and hungry. Have a mild case of the squitters. Seventy-five per cent of the men are sick. The camp covers quite a large area. There are 40,000 P.O.W.s here. The camp is divided into compounds, each holding about 5,000 men. In our compound there are 1,400 from the Royal Air Forces of Canada, Australia, South Africa and Britain; 1,000 U.S. Army officers; 1,000 Polish Army officers, and civilian Polish Jews.

Directly north of our compound, separated from us by barbed wire, were British Army N.C.O.s and privates, also French and Serb working parties.

To the west and adjoining us were Norwegians, 1,700 Navy and Army officers. They were very friendly and honest and had a great sense of humour. We visited and exchanged food and cigarettes through the barbed wire fence. The majority of them spoke fluent English and I enjoyed talking with them. They had many stories to tell about Gestapo atrocities they had witnessed.

To the south, and separated from us by parade grounds, were 3,000 American Army enlisted men. They lived in tents which, in the dead of German winter, must have been pretty grim.

We were constantly hungry. Most of our time was spent talking and dreaming about food. Our daily rations were as follows:

Morning - Unsweetened goon tea.

Mid-day - Cup of soup with two or three potatoes.

Evening - One-seventh of a loaf of bread, margarine and goon tea.

We were counted twice daily on the parade grounds. The rest of the time we were free to roam around inside our compounds.

I struck up a friendship with a Polish Jew who was mere skin and bones. He weighed well under 100 pounds and his most noticeable feature was his eyes; they reflected so much sorrow, pain and suffering. He was an accomplished artist and for a few cigarettes he agreed to pencil my portrait and do a drawing of the Halifax bomber I flew on my final mission. I have them to this day, stored in my P.O.W. log book.

Early in April 1945, the Russian Army was reported to be making great advances in our direction. It was assumed the capture of Berlin was their goal and to get there they would have to pass our camp at Lukenwald.

On 20th April, the German guards disappeared during the night. The following day news bulletins kept us in

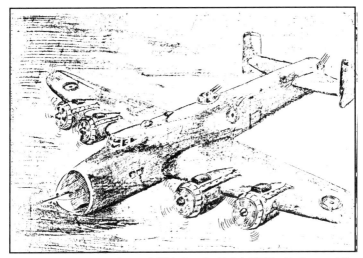
Halifax bomber drawn in my POW diary by Polish POW at Lukenwald in exchange for a cigarette.

touch with the position of the Russians and what was happening in Lukenwald. We heard that a train had arrived from Berlin and the soldiers were evacuating. S.S. officers told the Senior British Commander that any prisoner leaving the camp at night would be shot. Eight rifles had been stolen and were demanded back by the Germans. They were returned quickly so that no reprisals would take place.

Next day Lukenwald was shelled by the Russians. Reports arrived that the German military had pulled out of Lukenwald, which was now being defended by a home guard of old men and young boys. The Russians were getting nearer and nearer at every report. April 22nd was a Sunday. Around 1000 hours they arrived.

The first evidence of Russians we saw was a well-camouflaged tank that drove completely around the camp ripping down the barbed wire fence and destroying the goon towers with well-placed cannon rounds. After completing its circuit of the camp, the tank came to a halt near the homemade Union Jack and Stars and Stripes we had made from sheets and odd pieces of cloth and prominently displayed in the compound's centre.

When the access hatch of the tank opened, we were surprised to see Mongolian soldiers clambering out. There were many more of them than one would have expected a tank to hold. They wore no uniforms and their civilian clothes were in worse condition than our P.O.W. clothing.

Their attitude was rather hostile, definitely not friendly. My first impression was that by losing the Germans and gaining the Russians we had jumped from the frying pan into the fire.

An interpreter was found and we discovered they wanted us to follow them and help kill the Germans. Through the interpreter our Senior Officer pointed out that we were airmen and had not been trained as soldiers. The Russians then reluctantly took off in a very foul mood.

Shortly after the departure of the tank the Mayor of Lukenwald arrived and invited us to move into town. Then crowds of women, old and young, arrived with the same invitation. This invitation was extended not through civility or affection but because they were scared to death of the Russians and hoped our presence in town would keep them away.

They had every right to fear the Russians. The Russian P.O.W.s had been cruelly treated as slave labour. The Germans had worked and starved them until they had died by the thousands. After they were liberated, many roamed around killing and raping as they pleased.

Two of my P.O.W. buddies and I moved into a comfortable apartment in town. Ray Watts, an Australian, had been a navigator on a Lancaster bomber; Cy Grant, from Trinidad, had been the pilot of a Mosquito bomber. We had been in town a week when one of our German neighbours arrived at our door in a very excited state. There was an American Army truck in the Town Square, she told us, parked near the *Bergermeister's* office. The driver of the truck was black and she had never seen a black man before. This obviously contributed to her state of excitement.

Ray, Cy and I grabbed our kit bags and ran to the square. Sure enough, there was the truck. It was already almost full of P.O.W.s. The two U.S. Army corporals in charge had made the mistake of getting lost and crossing a pontoon bridge into Russian-occupied territory. The Russians had refused to let them cross back.

We persuaded the corporals to make a run for it and climbed into the crowded back of the truck. We hoped the Russians would not dare fire on an ally. They did try to stop us as we approached the bridge by waving their machine guns around. We ignored them and, in the end, they waved us onto the pontoon bridge and we made it to the safety of American-occupied territory on the other side.

On arrival at U.S. Army Headquarters we were given a royal welcome, followed by a great meal. We were given toiletry items and were able to get ourselves deloused, scrubbed squeaky clean, and into new underwear and clothes.

The following day we were flown in a DC-3 to Louvaine, in Belgium. There we were checked into a hospital for a week of medical tests and fed so well it was obvious they wanted us to regain all the weight we had lost before we were returned to England.

From Louvaine we were flown to an aerodrome in the south of England, then on to the R.C.A.F. Headquarters in Bournemouth. There we underwent a thorough medical examination and several debriefings. I was able to collect my clothes, uniforms and personal items I had left at the Squadron, as well as my R.C.A.F. pilot's log book that has been so valuable to me in the writing of these memoirs.

We were told we had top priority for return to Canada. True to their word, a few days later I boarded a large cruise ship, the *SS Louis Pasteur,* along with hundreds of ex-P.O.W.s and the wives and children of Canadian servicemen. We travelled in comfort and had the best of everything; it was so different from my trip over to England on the *Queen Mary.*

On arrival in Montreal I was instructed to report to the R.C.A.F. station located in Lachine, Quebec. I had another medical check and was booked onto a P.B.Y. flying boat to Nassau via Bermuda. I had been granted three week's leave, after which I had to report back to Lachine. After an overnight layover in Bermuda, I made the final leg of the long trek from Lukenwald to Nassau.

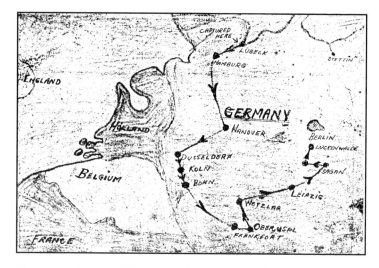

My odyssey through POW camps in Germany. I drew this map in my POW diary.

CHAPTER 14

HOME AGAIN

After a few days with my mother and father and visiting friends I was glad to get away with Mary and our little son, Leonard Jr., for two weeks at a seaside cottage on Cable Beach in west Nassau. All too soon the weeks went by and it was time to move back with Mom and Dad for the last week of my vacation.

I wanted to forget the war and all the horrible things I had seen and been a part of. So many of my friends were dead and already forgotten by the greedy people they died for.

Unfortunately some of my friends, and in particular my Dad, did not appreciate my reluctance to talk about my flying experiences. I deeply regret that I hurt his feelings by not being more understanding and willing to share my experiences with him. He was always bragging to his friends about his four sons who had served in the armed forces, referred to by Hon. Etienne Dupuch's *Tribune* as "the fighting Thompsons."

My first playtime with my son, Leonard Jr. (Cable Beach, Nassau 1946).

He would end his remarks by saying that he only wanted the Good Lord to spare his life until all of his boys were home from war, then he would be ready to go. True to his prediction, he did pass away one week after his eldest and youngest sons had returned from England. His early, senseless death at the age of 56 was caused by the wrong blood type being administered while he was being treated for a bleeding ulcer.

Dad had been suffering from this condition for some time. He was being treated by our family doctor, Dr. K. Rogers, who suggested a transfusion was necessary. An appointment was made but on the day of the transfusion we received a message from Dr. Roger's office saying the doctor was off the island and as a result a visiting Canadian doctor would fill in for him.

Dad was out for a walk with my son perched on his shoulders when the doctor arrived. We found him and took him to his bedroom where the transfusion would be performed. My elder brother Hartis and I were with him along with the donor, who seemed very nervous. "Don't worry about it," Dad tried to reassure him. "Just imagine what I'll be like after getting your young blood into me!"

Within seconds of starting the transfusion Dad was having a problem breathing. The doctor immediately discontinued the transfusion and asked Hartis to go with him. They were barely out of the room when Dad whispered: "Leonard, I'm dying. I am not afraid. Promise me I will get a Catholic burial." The next moment he was gone.

The doctor and Hartis returned about ten minutes later with an oxygen tank, too late to save Dad's life. We discovered later that the donor's blood had never been matched or tested with Dad's.

His request for a Catholic burial was the result of him having converted to that faith a few years earlier. It had been a sore point with my mother who remained a faithful Methodist.

I saw to it that Dad received a Catholic burial in the Western Cemetery of Nassau. The Methodists refused my mother's request for a burial plot at her church, so when my mother passed on we buried her next to Dad.

A few days before my departure for Canada I was offered a position by Andy of John S. George, a hardware store in Nassau. I was also offered the chance to be a civil aviation pilot by my old teacher, George Morley, who was now the General Manager of Bahamas Air, a wholly owned subsidiary of Pan American Airways. Needless to say, it was a very easy choice for me to make as I was itching to get airborne again.

On arrival back at Lachine I had a final medical and signed many documents. Unfortunately, many of the veteran benefits were unavailable outside Canada but the R.C.A.F. officials were as generous and helpful as possible. I have nothing but the highest regard and respect for all the Canadian officers and airmen I served with from April 1940 to June 1945. Even today the Canadian people and government honour their veterans and support their organisations more than any other country I know of. I attended several P.O.W. conventions and, most recently, the 50th Anniversary of Squadron 426 at Trenton, Ontario.

Matters were very different in The Bahamas. One of our amateur politicians was asked what the government intended to do for servicemen returning from the European theatre. "They didn't have to go," he replied. "Give them a cutlass and lease them an acre of land–That's more than they deserve." I had to hang my head in shame.

I went to Montreal and sat an examination for a Commercial Pilot's Licence which I passed without too much trouble. This enabled me to start flying as soon as I arrived back in Nassau. Later, on the strength of my Canadian licence, I was issued the second-ever Bahamian Transport Pilot's Licence.

I commenced flying with Bahamas Air as a co-pilot for the sum of fifteen pounds a week. The fleet at this stage consisted of one twin engine 22-seat Consolidated Commodore flying boat, the same type of plane Pan Am had used on its Miami-Nassau-Havana run.

The pilot, Captain Peen, was a New Zealander who had migrated to Canada and spent many years flying in the North West Territory. He realised that it was only a matter of time before this "young, inexperienced, reckless wartime pilot" (as he constantly referred to me) would replace him. He was therefore reluctant to let me take my turn flying the aeroplane and regularly denigrated R.C.A.F. pilots in the presence of our passengers.

All this suddenly changed one Sunday morning. We took off early for Harbour Island with a full complement of passengers. Halfway to Eleuthera we encountered a long line of squalls with towering thunderheads and fierce lightning. Dark clouds went down to sea level.

It became obvious that Capt. Peen intended to fly straight into this mess. I suggested we should skirt along the outside of the storm and look for a weak spot to fly through. "Just what I would expect from you," he commented and continued on course. As he was speaking I noticed a disturbance on the surface of the water that indicated the beginnings of a waterspout touch-down. We were headed straight for it. I tightened my seatbelt firmly and, as I did so, noticed that Capt. Peen was not wearing his.

Before I could say anything there was a tremendous bang like a clap of thunder and we were carried up sharply with the altimeter spinning like a top. Just as suddenly we were heading down with Capt. Peen glued to the roof. We broke out of the clouds about 200 feet off the water with me hanging onto the controls and slowly opening the throttles that Capt. Peen had closed when we first hit the updraught.

Shortly afterwards, we were out of the storm and into beautiful sunlight. I unbuckled my belt and went to check on the passengers, noticing as I went that Capt. Peen was bleeding from a cut on his head.

On entering the cabin from the cockpit I noticed the smell of acid. There was a navigation table on the starboard side that housed two large 24 volt batteries beneath, that were used to operate the radio. The batteries were lying upside down in the passageway and the two passengers in this compartment were both in a daze, one of them bleeding profusely from a head cut. The other compartments were not so bad. Most of the passengers had been wearing their seatbelts and had escaped serious injury. As I returned to my seat I noticed that all the hinged inspection covers on the underside of the wings were open and flapping in the slipstream created by the 104 foot wingspan.

We landed at Harbour Island and, after all the passengers disembarked, Capt. Peen and I went ashore to check with Dr. Tudhope on the status of the injured passengers. Three of them had received stitches and, from all reports, it seemed nobody would be flying back with us. We then went for lunch at Miss Hattie's little boarding house where we discussed the flight.

Capt. Peen was so friendly I couldn't believe it. He promised to let me fly the plane back to Nassau and said he would suggest to Mr. Morley that I take the aircraft out for an hour of take offs and landings. He added that it might be expedient not to mention to Mr. Morley the difficulties we had experienced on the way over. I told him I had no intention of saying anything to Mr. Morley but I would bet my last dollar he had already received a dozen calls from Harbour Island.

We took off late in the afternoon with only two passengers. After landing at Nassau I suggested to Capt. Peen that the aircraft should be hauled up on the ramp for a check. I feared that the battery acid had gone down into the bilge and would eat holes in the aluminium skin. He pooh-poohed this, no doubt not wanting to draw attention to the matter.

Next morning I noticed something seemed different about the Commodore. Then it came to me–she was riding low in the water. I went on board and discovered several feet of water in the cabin and all the seat cushions floating around. On further investigation I found that many of the rivets that held the bottom aluminium skin to the metal frame had dropped out and I could look straight through the aircraft to the sea bottom. Only the sponsons on each side of the seaplane had prevented it from sinking. At least the cockpit instruments and radio and cable controls were well above water.

The Commodore was hauled up a special ramp and a full inspection carried out. Oversized rivets replaced those that had fallen out.

Our schedule in those days was not a busy one. Few people could afford to charter us and most of our flights were on a scheduled basis for which we received a subsidy from the government for carrying the mail. At this time our schedule comprised two weekly trips on Fridays and Sundays to Harbour Island. Later this was expanded to take in Governor's Harbour and Rock Sound. There were no airports in the Out Islands then so we had to remain on the water until departure time when we would retrace our outward route back to Nassau.

Once a month we flew to Georgetown, Exuma; Hope Town, Marsh Harbour and Green Turtle Cay, on Abaco; and West End, Grand Bahama. In between flights we carried out maintenance, which was considerably more extensive than on regular aircraft because of the corrosive effects of salt water.

Flying was still a novelty in those days and crowds would gather to watch our take offs and landings, particularly on a Sunday or a holiday. Our arrival in the Out Is-

The Grumman Goose and Commodore docked on the P.A.A. ramp, Nassau, in 1946.

Loading the Commodore at the P.A.A. Dock in Nassau for a trip to Harbour Island. Nigel Marix is on the dock and I am standing over the passenger entrance to the Commodore.

This P.B.Y. Amphibian was converted to a 22-passenger plane and was used by Bahamas Airways from 1947 to 1965.

lands would bring out the entire population. Sometimes I would 'buzz' a settlement before landing so they could all get down to the beach or harbour to watch the spectacle.

After Capt. Peen left I was the sole pilot for about six months. When Capt. Collar was released from the Naval Air Force he returned and assumed the role of Managing Pilot. Our fleet was increased by two Grumman amphibious aircraft and one PBY 5A Catalina amphibian. The Catalina had been widely used during the war for submarine patrols and air sea rescue operations. Our aircraft had been extensively modified and fitted with 22 seats.

Our staff was increased by the addition of a pilot named Adam Kalkowsky. He had been flying for Pan Am at the outbreak of the Pacific hostilities and had been taken prisoner by the Japanese in Manila. After hearing some of his stories I considered myself lucky to have been taken prisoner in Germany. A mechanic named Bob Addison arrived with Capt. Collar, and Jack Graham, an ex-R.A.F. Englishman, came aboard as mechanic and flight engineer for the PBY. Jack had been stationed in Nassau during the war and had married a Bahamian girl.

Capt. Collar (Charlie, as I called him) was determined to make a go of Bahamas Air and he found work for the aircraft that no one had dreamed of. One of his most profitable charters was a deal with Cayman Airways to serve the Caymans from Kingston. Bobby Owen Roberts was the operator of Cayman Airways and he had a contract with the British government to provide the service.

Adam and I took turns on this charter for a month at a time with Jack as engineer. At the end of the month we would fly back to Nassau for maintenance and checks and a change of pilots, but poor Jack had to stay with the aircraft all the time.

The route was from Kingston to Montego Bay, then on to Cayman Brac where we flew low over the island and dropped the mail bag out of the old camera hatch in the rear of the aircraft. We then landed at Grand Cayman in a protected bay. We quickly discharged and took on passengers for Tampa, Florida, where we usually arrived well after dark.

The following morning we would retrace our route back to Palisades Airport, Kingston, arriving around nine in the evening.

Sometimes finding the Cayman Islands could be a problem as there were no navigational facilities on the island with the exception of a telegraph station that operated infrequently. When the weather was bad the telegraph station might listen in for a call from us. The pilot would call in Morse code, not an easy feat to do while controlling a plane in bad weather, and the station operator would hold down his key giving us a constant signal. From this we would try to establish a bearing. This bearing on the station was not always accurate in bad weather as it could be thrown off by static electricity. In these circumstances we would fly beyond our expected time of arrival and then do a 'square search'. No one ever failed to find and land at Grand Cayman as the PBY had tremendous range and the ability to fly for twelve hours.

There was little employment in the Caymans in those days and many of the men shipped out as merchant seamen using Tampa as a base. This was the reason we had Tampa on our schedule.

In Kingston we stayed at a very old but posh hotel, the Myrtle Bank, situated in the centre of town. The hotel restaurant was famed for its great food and insisted on coat and tie for the evening meal.

One evening I was dressing for supper when Jack arrived already prepared. "Your room is bigger than mine," he commented as he looked around. "You even have a water fountain." Water fountain? I thought to myself. Then I heard a splash and a choking sound come from the bathroom. I rushed in to find Jack bending over the bidet, soaking wet. He had never seen a bidet before. I laughed until I cried, and so did Jack when I explained the real use of the 'water fountain' to him.

Some time after our charter contract had expired and we were back in Nassau, Bobby Roberts was killed on take off from Palisades Airport. He had done so much for the people of the Cayman Islands and was responsible for putting the little colony on the map. A few years after his death an airport was built at George Town, Grand Cayman, and named the Owen Roberts Airport in appreciation of his great contribution to the islands.

CHAPTER 15

FLYING THE ISLANDS

After almost two years with Bahamas Airways I became very disillusioned and quit when I discovered that the three foreign pilots were making almost double my salary. I know that Capt. Collar and George Morley had gone to bat for me. My enemy, apparently, was Sidney Farrington, a Bahamian and a Director of Pan American Airways. For some reason this type of person could not stand to see a fellow Bahamian make good, particularly if he was from one of the Out Islands. More about this attitude later on.

A week after leaving Bahamas Airways I commenced flying with Colyn Rees who owned Nassau Aviation and operated a Grumman Goose and Widgeon. Colyn was an ex-R.A.F. pilot who had served with Ferry Command. He had ferried aircraft from Nassau down through the West Indies and South America then across to Ascension Island, a long flight over open water. From there he would fly on to destinations in Africa and sometimes even to Calcutta in eastern India.

After a short time with Colyn and Nassau Aviation I returned to Bahamas Airways at the urging of Capt. Collar and George Morley. Sidney Farrington no longer had a voice in the company and my salary was brought into line with the foreign pilots.

The charter business increased steadily and for some time we were hard pressed to meet the demand. Two major oil companies, Shell and Superior Oil, were exploring and drilling for oil in Andros and they provided us with plenty of business.

We moved all of our amphibian aircraft to Oakes

I flew with Nassau Aviation in this Grumman Widgeon.

Field and only used the Pan American ramp for the Commodore, which was close to being retired.

To help out during the busy winter season Cliff Kernochan, a friend of Capt. Collar, arrived with his Widgeon. Cliff flew exclusively for Averell Harriman during the summer months flying him from his home on Long Island, New York, to his office downtown. He would land on the Hudson River and taxi up a ramp right in the heart of Wall Street. Cliff, his wife Dottie, and his two children, Hoopy and Linda, were a great addition to the ever-growing circle of pilots and mechanics and their families associated with Bahamas Airways. We all looked forward to their arrival in Nassau each year. Cliff bought a house on Cable Beach and returned year after year until his untimely death shortly after he retired from flying. Dottie still comes to Nassau each year and is very active in social and church activities.

Early in 1949 Capt. Collar was involved in two accidents that I am sure had a bearing on his decision to retire from flying and leave The Bahamas. The first accident was caused by him trying to land a Widgeon amphibian aircraft in the waters off Hope Town with the undercarriage in the down position. The Widgeon flipped over on its back but nobody was injured.

It was discovered that there was a malfunction in the hydraulic system. The landing gear would not lock, and when the flaps were selected down prior to landing the landing gear also came down. Grumman accepted full responsibility and replaced the aircraft, thereby absolving Capt. Collar of all blame.

The second accident followed shortly after this incident. Capt. Collar and a mechanic had gone out late in the afternoon to assist with one of our aircraft that had mechanical problems. On return to Nassau he found the airport closed due to a heavy rainstorm. He decided to land in the water on the south side of New Providence and wait for the airport to open.

By the time word came through that the airport was open, it was quite dark. As the aircraft attempted to take off it hit a barely submerged rock and suffered extensive damage. Fortunately, Capt. Collar and the mechanic escaped with a few minor cuts. Not long after this he was offered a position with the Federal Aviation Authority as an aircraft accident inspector for Florida and the Caribbean.

I was sorry to see Capt. Collar leave Bahamas Airways. He was the best pilot I ever knew and did so much to help my own flying career. I often see him at his home in Coral Gables, Florida, where he went to live after retiring.

As it turned out, Capt. Collar left Bahamas Airways at a propitious time. A few months after his departure the Bahamas government persuaded Pan Am to sell Bahamas Airways to British South American Airways. A few months after the acquisition by B.S.A.A. the company suffered two fatal accidents, one right after the other.

The more serious accident occurred after the aircraft had taken off from Bermuda on its way to South America. The pilot called in to say he had reached cruising altitude and all was well. There was no further contact. The press was quick to make the plane's disappearance part of the "Bermuda Triangle" mystery. The resultant bad publicity forced British South American Airways out of business and British Overseas Airways Corporation stepped in to take over Bahamas Airways.

Shortly after the takeover I was promoted to Managing Pilot. I still flew as many hours as the other pilots but had a lot of desk work in addition. My Commercial Manager was Harold Woodman, my dearest friend. He had come to The Bahamas with the R.A.F. and married a local girl. My secretary was Alice Waugh. She knew how much I hated having a desk job and worked hard to keep my paperwork to the minimum. Whenever I flew I knew the company was in the capable hands of Harold and Alice.

The company was now 65 strong and even had a Financial Controller, Mr. Gallo, who was on loan from B.O.A.C. I have aways looked upon accountants as a necessary evil, but Mr. Gallo's performance persuaded me otherwise.

The Bahamas Air Ways crew consisted of Thompson as managing pilot, Galo as accountant (standing on left), the chief mechanic, and Harold Woodman as commercial manager.

We were often called upon to make emergency night flights to the Out Islands. Sometimes a doctor or nurse would accompany us but mostly we were alone with the patients unless a family member accompanied them into Nassau. Most of the calls came to me so I did many of these dangerous night flights.

Not all of the flights were real emergencies. There is no doubt that many lives were saved by getting patients into the hospital in Nassau for prompt treatment, but it is equally true that many patients could have waited until daylight.

I give as an example the case of a lady from Hope Town, the wife of a good friend of mine. I received a marine radio call from her husband at about ten o' clock one night. According to him, his wife was in urgent need of a doctor and would not last the night. I pointed out that the weather was very bad in Nassau but he pleaded with me and I finally relented.

I instructed him to check the area outside the harbour for a distance of three miles downwind. He was then to return upwind about halfway to the harbour and anchor. When he heard me fly over he was to place a light in the bow of the boat and two lights in the stern, one on each side. This would give me the direction of the wind and a position I must not go beyond if I had not already touched down.

I took off from Oakes Field at 11 p.m. I ran into light rain and even though I was flying at 1500 feet I could see no land. I flew for twenty minutes beyond my E.T.A. then made a 180 degree turn to a reciprocal heading. I saw the surf of heavy seas breaking on the shoreline that I recognised as Whale Cay, about 20 miles north of Hope Town. From there it was easy to find Hope Town.

In those days there was no electricity in the Out Islands and when people went to bed they put out their oil lamps. Dark as it was, landing on the water did not present a great problem if one was familiar with the area and the wind direction and distance from the shoreline were established. There was always the possibility of flying into an obstacle such as the unlighted mast of a sailboat, however, and that was why I had the area checked out.

I anchored as soon as possible after landing, to avoid taxiing in the dark. I did not have long to wait before they arrived. The woman appeared to be in great pain so I wasted no time in taking off for Nassau. I breathed a sigh of relief as we loaded her into the waiting ambulance. I thanked God she had not died on route.

Imagine my surprise when my friend arrived at my house early next morning with a big smile on his face. "You are not going to believe this," he told me, "but all the way to the hospital, the missus was letting wind like crazy and the pain disappeared. The doctor says there's nothing wrong with her, it was just gas pains."

When we received an emergency call we would drop everything, often leaving a half-eaten meal on the table, exceed the speed limit on the way to the airport, then take off and cruise at maximum settings. On arrival at our destination we would buzz the settlement and land near any small boat that might be anchored near the shore or drawn up on the beach. Sometimes we had to wade or swim ashore to supervise the ferrying of the patient out to the seaplane. Believe it or not, there were times when the person who brought the patient to the aircraft expected the pilot to pay him in cash for his pains! Thank goodness this attitude existed in only a few of the islands.

Another emergency flight that stands out vividly in my mind concerned my brother, Roscoe, and his friend, Lou Dictro, who had gone to Sandy Point for the weekend. They both had too much to drink and on their way back to their boat late at night they decided to take a short cut across somebody's back yard. Lou stumbled and fell into a well, breaking his leg in the process.

Roscoe called me around midnight and suggested I pick them up as soon as possible as Lou was in great pain. He assured me he would personally check the landing area and be ready by the time I arrived.

And ready he was. With the help of many of his Sandy Point friends there were ten or twelve boats anchored one behind the other in a straight line, all well lit with lanterns. As a result, landing and taking off presented no problems–very different from my usual night landings. It was just as safe as landing on a well-lit runway at a busy airport.

A few nights later, back in Nassau, Roscoe and Lou were at the Spider Web Night Club that Roscoe owned. George Symonette, a famous Bahamian entertainer, was playing there at the time. When Roscoe explained to George why Lou was on crutches, he went over to his piano and began to sing:

Did you see Uncle Lou when he fell in the well?
Oh, Oh, Uncle Lou, when he fell in the well;
I was standing there when he fell in the well...
He fell so far he went straight to hell...
Oh, oh, Uncle Lou, when he fell in the well...

We continued to expand our scheduled flights to not only include Abaco, Eleuthera, Exuma and Grand Bahama but also Havana and Santiago in Cuba, and Montego Bay and Kingston, Jamaica. In addition we ran scheduled flights to Miami and West Palm Beach. Our fleet consisted of five DC-3s, two 2O passenger P.B.Y.s, four Grumman Goose and two Grumman Widgeons, the latter only for charter duties.

Our inaugural flight to West Palm Beach was a public relations disaster. The flight had been widely announced and invitations hand-delivered to the Mayor of Palm Beach, many of the socialites of the area, travel agents and such.

We were scheduled for a ten o'clock departure in a PBY. Our agent and the news media were informed we would be arriving at West Palm Beach at 11:30. Our Chairman, Sir Harold Christie, was late as usual. I thought that, by rushing the take off and avoiding detours because of weather conditions, we might still make our E.T.A. This was not to be. Shortly after take off Sir Harold sent me a note saying we had to pick up Mr. Wasey, the principal owner of Cat Cay. It turned out that Mr. Wasey had not been informed of this invitation so we had to wait while he prepared himself for the trip.

A Bahamas Airways Grumman Goose that was used for charters in 1950 and myself.

We arrived in West Palm Beach two hours late and there was, of course, no one to meet us. The dignitaries had all left in disgust. The crowning of this farce was that the passengers had to stay in the aircraft for another half an hour. The drop from the aircraft to the ground was very high and our West Palm Beach agent, Nigel Marx, had arranged to borrow steps from a local airline. Once we were late, the steps were put back into use elsewhere. From then on the DC-3s were used for all of our foreign scheduled flights.

On our late flights to Kingston and Miami we overnighted. One of the stewardesses told me that our crews were frequenting a night club near Miami Airport that was a hang out for the gay crowd, and that one of our pilots had a crush on one of them. I was anxious to investigate this for myself and it so happened I had to go over to Miami with our Chief Mechanic, Red Woodburn, to check one of our aircraft that was over there to have its interior refurbished.

When Red and I arrived at the night club we discovered our errant pilot dancing cheek to cheek with the most beautiful blonde I have ever seen. She was really well-built

A Bahamas Airways Grumman Goose and me.

and both Red and I wondered if the stewardess had made a mistake.

At the end of the dance, as the couple started towards our table, Red whispered to me: "I'm going to find out if she's real!" As she was being introduced to Red, he quickly pinched her breast. At this point all hell broke loose. The 'lady' swung her pocket book at Red and in the ensuing fight her beautiful hair came off, along with several other items of clothing that left no doubt our girl was a boy. We beat a hasty retreat.

"Why on earth did you do that?" I demanded of Red once we were outside.

Red grinned. "If she was for real when I pinched her she should have said 'Ouch!'"

Our pilot was heartbroken and very embarrassed. He swore he had no idea there was anything wrong and that his 'girl friend' had always discouraged attempts at physical intimacy.

From 1946 to 1956 a fine group of pilots, the early pioneers in Bahamian aviation, gave the country a safe and dependable air service at no cost to Bahamian tax payers. As a matter of fact, for the last five years of my service with Bahamas Airways the company showed a small profit each year.

Besides myself, there was Philip Farrington from The Bahamas; Charlie, Cliff Kernochan, Dick McNally, Adam Kalkowsky, Jimmy Sproull, Joe Hettel, Roger Stewart and Gil Hensler from the United States; Johnny Whitehead and Tubby Welch from England; Don Douglas from Canada, John Roberts from St. Lucia and, last but not least, Colyn Rees from Bermuda.

CHAPTER 16

TREASURE CAY

On my first flight to Abaco after joining Bahamas Airways in 1945 I looked down on the beautiful beach at Sand Bank Cays as I flew over and it brought back boyhood memories and my dreams for a resort there. Whenever I flew near without passengers I would divert and circle the area, dreaming of the great potential for this pristine crescent beach.

On one occasion I had a charter for Billy (later Sir William) Butlin of the famous Butlin Holiday Camps in England. We left Nassau with his lawyer, Sir Stafford Sands, and party for West Palm Beach via Abaco and West End, Grand Bahama. Billy Butlin was looking for a site on which to build a holiday camp in The Bahamas. I immediately thought of Sand Banks.

It was a beautiful day and as we crossed Abaco I went to great pains to stay at the right distance and height to present as perfect a picture as possible of the flawless beach. Billy Butlin sat on my right in the co-pilot's seat and appeared to show interest. We then went on to our next destination, an aerial inspection of West End.

When I dropped Billy Butlin and his party off in West Palm Beach he said, "Thank you for a good flight, Captain. I couldn't help but notice you gave us a great view of that property in Abaco. I wonder why you didn't do the same at West End?" He must have noticed my guilty look for he smiled and added: "I agree with you. Abaco has more to offer. But I want to be in a place that's a $14 air fare from Florida."

An aerial view of Treasure Cay just after starting its development in 1957.

Shortly thereafter he built his camp at West End. Midet Aviation and later Mackey Airlines operated daily flights to West End from Miami and West Palm Beach for $14 round trip.

I discovered that most of the Sand Banks property was owned by the Crown. There were several areas bordering the property to the north and west that were privately owned and I made arrangements to buy them. I then found out that the Crown Agents had entered into a lease agreement with a Canadian, Major Bell. At this stage I thought my dream would never be realised.

Months later I was scheduled to fly a party to one of the Out Islands. The departure was set for 5 a.m., around daylight, in order to give the maximum amount of time at the destination. On the evening before the flight Mr. Rudy Sweetnam, the Crown Lands surveyor, called to say he would have to leave later as he had nowhere to get breakfast at that hour. I invited him to breakfast with me and that was the beginning of a friendship that I cherished until his untimely death.

Born and raised in British Guiana, he was one of the most honest and sincere gentlemen I have ever had the pleasure to know. On occasion we would discuss politics and race relations in The Bahamas. He had been surprised when I invited him for breakfast. Until that time he had never been invited into a white man's house.

Of course, I told him all about my dreams for Sand Bank Cays and sometime later I was told that Major Bell was dead and his family was not interested in continuing the lease. I immediately applied to Mr. Sweetnam to lease the property. Some time later I was given a conditional lease purchase for a period of five years with the right to a further period of five years, provided the conditions of the first period were met. The conditions were extremely tough and I suspected that my friendship with Rudy had been a disadvantage for me. He obviously wanted nobody to be able to say I had received special consideration.

The lease payments amounted to several thousand dollars a year. I had to erect five permanent buildings, including a forty room hotel, as well as construct a golf course, lay down roads, and do extensive dredging and landscaping. All this would cost in excess of five million dollars. When all this had been completed to the satisfaction of the Crown Lands officer, I then had the right to purchase the property for the sum of eight pounds an acre–more than I had paid for the private property with no improvements necessary. This will no doubt come as a surprise to some of my so-called friends who constantly raise the question of the "free" land I acquired from Crown at Sand Banks Cays.

During the first few years of the lease I had trouble finding the cash to pay the annual lease fees. I had prepared a catalogue of photographs from the ground and air, and wherever I went I would approach likely investors with the idea of financing my dream. I was still busy flying in those days and came in contact with the rich and famous on a daily basis. I solicited several of them, including Clint Murcheson and Bob Hope. Clint Murcheson was then the owner of the Dallas Cowboys football team. While I failed to interest him in Sand Banks Cays I did introduce him to Spanish Cay, which he later bought and developed.

There was no airport at Sand Banks nor any road to Marsh Harbour. I had to fly prospective investors to the area in a seaplane and, after landing, taxi as close to the beach as possible. I would anchor there and we would wade ashore to make the inspection. Most of the people I persuaded to take advantage of a free inspection flight were good sports from old money, but had no imagination or desire to invest.

In the case of Bob Hope, after anchoring close to shore I jumped from the plane into about three feet of water. "Here's where you get out," I called to him. "Use belly for boat!"

Instead of jumping, he stood in the doorway with a pained expression. "I'm not getting in there with all those sharks," he told me. "I can see the beautiful beach from where I'm standing."

Two years went by so quickly, almost half of the first portion of my lease. I had wined and dined so many likely prospects, all to no avail. Then, from out of the blue, came the most promising prospect yet.

I had flown to Dallas to inspect a DC-3 aircraft that I wished to purchase for Skyways, my new company for scheduled flights in The Bahamas. The owner of the DC-3, Mr. Wyatt C. Hedrick, was a well-known architect. Shortly after the purchase was complete I went to work with my pictures and plans of Sand Bank Cays, stressing the charm and beauty of Abaco. Tom Stanley, a partner of Mr. Hedrick's, overheard my presentation. He was impressed and thought that he knew someone who might be interested in financing my dream. In addition, he would prepare preliminary plans for developing the property. It was further agreed that if he was successful he would be given ten percent of the shares in the developing company. By the time I left Dallas, Tom had completed the initial development plan, which I was able to take back with me to Nassau.

Early in 1958, several months after I had first met Tom, he came to Nassau with Dumas Milner, a self-made millionaire from Jackson, Mississippi. He was a real estate developer as well as the largest General Motors dealer in the U.S. We flew in Dumas' plane to Marsh Harbour, then hired a boat to take us to Sand Banks.

After inspecting the property Tom and Dumas were both very impressed and anxious to form a partnership and get moving with the development. A legal partnership was entered into with Dumas holding the position of Chairman of the Board responsible for financing the scheme. Tom Stanley would be a director responsible for development and I would be the managing director. It would be my job to pave the way with government permits, hire local labour, and deal with local issues.

The new company was called Dumas Milner (Bahamas) Ltd. Later on this was changed to Treasure Cay Ltd. Before Dumas and Tom left Nassau it was agreed that the funds for trucks, bulldozers and other items of equipment needed to clear roads in preparation for building would be on hand in a matter of days.

I had a lease payment due so you can imagine my dismay as the weeks, then months, went by with no word from Dumas or Tom. Eventually, after six months, they arrived with a banker who had agreed to loan Dumas Milner (Bahamas) Ltd. one million dollars, subject to inspecting the property. Within a few days after their departure the promised funds arrived. I was soon to find that everything we purchased in the U.S. through Dumas Milner was financed, down to the smallest item.

In the earliest stages of the development financing was arranged and guaranteed by Dumas. Later on the land we had acquired from the Crown was used as collateral for development loans. Our financing was always slow in coming so we were never able to follow our original development plan and move from stage to stage automatically.

Dumas had many irons in the fire in the States and his visits were few and far between. When he did come it was usually to entertain some financier he was trying to interest in investing in Treasure Cay or one of his other business concerns. When the first investment loan came through it was barely enough to cover the loan and carry on for a little while. A pattern developed that invariably left me behind in payments to the local merchants who, of course, held me responsible.

The first thing we did was build a dock near the area called Rock Point. A small bunk house with a kitchen and dining room was erected nearby. Some of the staff had to live on boats moored at the dock and when the number of employees increased we rented a large houseboat. Then followed Rock Point House, a lovely two-storey building especially designed for entertaining important guests. Dumas and I lived there whenever we were in Treasure Cay. We were well looked after by my dear friend, Isabelle Bootle.

While all of this was taking place we were busy clearing land for the hotel site near the beach and pushing in roads. The building of a 40 room hotel was started, along with five two-bedroom cottages near the proposed marina. Every effort was made to speedily qualify under the terms of the lease agreement in order to purchase a portion of the property.

Late in 1959 the Crown Lands officer agreed that we had more than qualified under the terms of our agreement and we were able to purchase 460 acres, just under fifty per cent of the total lease.

By the early part of December 1961 the hotel was almost complete, so we set January 1st as the official opening date. The power and sewage plants were ready and we received a consignment of furniture and kitchen equipment from our West Palm Beach warehouse. Most of it was in place, but some still in packing crates outside the kitchen door, when disaster struck–FIRE!

It was shortly after midnight on December 19th when the alarm was raised. The fire had started in the mid-section of the building and, with little in the way of fire-fighting equipment, we could only watch as the hotel burned to the ground.

We were insured, of course, but the insurance company had not been notified that the furniture and kitchen equipment had been shipped to Sand Banks Cay so the company had to absorb the loss.

Treasure Cay–the beginning of a ten-year project.

We had no positive information as to how the fire started but I had reason to believe it was deliberately set by a yachtsman who had arrived a month previously. He and his wife caused us some problems and we had asked him to leave. He was seen near the hotel on the night of the fire and early next morning he took off. The police tried to locate him but had no success.

Our lease from Crown and all maps of the area referred to the property as Sand Banks Cay. We all felt that a more romantic name should be adopted. Because of the many stories of pirates and lost treasure in the area, I suggested the name Treasure Cay. It was unanimously agreed upon and the necessary steps to make it legal were carried out.

With no arterial roads on the mainland we had to run frequent shopping trips, and deal with occasional medical emergencies, by boat. All radio contact was by ship to shore marine transreceiver radio to another ship, Marsh Harbour, Nassau or Miami Marine.

Early in 1961 I was able to persuade Frank Christie, who served with me as one of Abaco's representatives in the

House of Assembly, to use his good offices to have government build a 2,500 foot runway on the mainland opposite Green Turtle Cay to serve the north end of Abaco. We agreed that Treasure Cay would add another 2,500 feet to the runway. We asked, in return, that the airport be named for Treasure Cay. By the time government had completed the first part of the runway we had put in a road from Treasure Cay to the airport.

When seeking permission from Crown Lands to construct the road from Treasure Cay to the airport, Mr. Sweetnam had warned me to follow the edge of the swamp and the green land in order to be clear of privately owned land. Unfortunately the bulldozer operator did not exactly follow instructions and in one or two areas he infringed on a few square feet of private property.

One man bitterly complained about this intrusion onto his property and threatened never to vote for me again. I felt disappointed because I had increased the value of his property a hundredfold and expected gratitude rather than grumpiness. Such is life.

Much later on, Owens Illinois drove a road from Marsh Harbour to the airport at Treasure Cay. They, too, shaved the same man's property but this time he did not complain.

In December of 1961 the first hotel at Treasure Cay burnt down just before its grand opening.

120

We subdivided a portion of the property and the sales went well, particularly the ocean front lots. This revenue was ploughed back into the development along with loans for specific projects. It was like pouring money into a bottomless pit. Six more houses were constructed on Ocean Boulevard and the dredging and other operations were instigated.

The creation of a marina near the hotel necessitated the dredging of a 3,000 foot long by 100 foot wide and 7 foot deep channel across a shallow mud flat. As a result a considerable amount of sand was dumped to one side of the channel, eventually creating a 64 acre island that later on we were able to purchase from the P.L.P. government at a grossly inflated price. This was certainly not the best way to encourage development.

We started the dredging with our own dredger specially purchased for this purpose. We soon found it was too small for the job. So I contacted an old friend, Ossie Moody, who had been in the business of dredging and marine construction for years. We were able to work out a contract for dredging and concrete sea walls. The dredging and construction of sea walls were soon finished to our complete satisfaction.

The second hotel was started early in 1962 on the same site as the original hotel. Fireproof concrete pre-cast slabs were used wherever possible. We made the mistake of using the same slabs for a flat roof and soon had to install a conventional roof to cover it because of leaks. The slabs had not been fastened properly, as we found out during Hurricane Betsy in 1965 when a portion of the roof blew off.

Dumas Milner was very friendly with Kimmons Wilson, the founder of the Holiday Inn chain of hotels. He frequently visited Treasure Cay and was anxious that we buy into his franchise. I thought the fee was exorbitant but Dumas had his way and we opened as the first Holiday Inn in The Bahamas.

This did not last very long. The benefits we received from Holiday Inn were not commensurate with our payments to be part of the chain.

The manager of the hotel was Jerry Melzer, a German national who had married a lovely girl, Cynthia, from Exuma. He had worked with me in Nassau as manager of Dirty Dick's Bar and Blackbeard's Tavern. I was very impressed with him and knew he had previous experience in hotel management. He was anxious to move out of Nassau and I thought he would be the answer for our hotel.

About the same time we needed someone with landscaping experience. The best person I knew was my own gardener, Moxey Williams, who was quite happy to make the move from Nassau to Abaco. He did a magnificent job of landscaping for us and I am pleased to say that over the years both he and Jerry Melzer have done extremely well in the business world and still reside in or near Treasure Cay.

Construction to rebuild the hotel at Treasure Cay began in 1962 on the same site as the first.

CHAPTER 17

ELBOW ROOM AND SKYWAYS

Several times a year the Managing Director of B.O.A.C. subsidiary companies would arrive in Nassau for a Board of Directors Meeting. The two local Board members were Sir Kenneth Solomon and Sir Harold Christie.

On one occasion I was complimented by Mr. Tony Snowball, the B.O.A.C. Subsidiary Director, who told me we were the only subsidiary owned by B.O.A.C. to show a regular profit. As a result he was going to recommend to the local board that my salary be increased, in line with other subsidiary managers, plus a company car for my personal use.

On the day of the meeting I accompanied the B.O.A.C. people downtown to Sir Kenneth's office where the meeting was to take place. I sat on the outside near a door that led into the office and could hear every word that was spoken.

When Tony Snowball finished relating his reasons for increasing my salary there was dead silence for almost a minute. Then Sir Kenneth spoke up. He said there was no way I should have my salary increased. The idea was absurd. He said he knew many people who had been managing stores in Nassau for years and didn't make anywhere near my salary. He went on and on and it was obvious he was very angry. As I walked away I recognised Sir Kenneth for what he really was and it came as no surprise that he and members of his circle did much towards destroying our lovely country.

Six months later I left Bahamas Airways and shortly thereafter started my own charter company, Skyway Bahamas Limited. My top staff all came over with me: Harold Woodman, Gil Hensler, Ed Albury and John Roberts. Just about all of the other pilots left for greener pastures. Don Douglas became Chief Pilot for a major Canadian oil company and Dick McNally Chief Pilot for Gulf Sulfur Company.

Peter Fair, an Englishman, arrived to manage Bahamas Airways. He was not a pilot. While I was Managing Pilot I flew most of the emergency flights and logged almost as many hours as the other pilots. What his salary was, I do not know. I do know the company rented a large house at Lyford Cay for him and also provided a chauffeur-driven car, a gardener and a considerable entertainment allowance. I assume Sir Kenneth and Sir Harold were frequent guests at his parties.

If my attitude seems peevish, I should point out that the ruling clique in Nassau at that time considered Out Island whites like myself to be "country bumpkins." They expected Abaco and Spanish Wells boys to arrive in Nassau and work as clerks for the rest of their lives for next to nothing. This was ironic for some of these men were of Out Island stock themselves and had only been in Nassau for a generation or so.

There was only one bank in Nassau at the time, the Royal Bank of Canada. No loan was made to a local Bahamian without first checking with Sir Kenneth. As a result, getting a start in business life was almost impossible for poor whites and blacks. Thank goodness this changed when Barclays, followed shortly by several other banks, opened branches in Nassau.

The next hurdle we had to overcome was getting a business licence and exchange control permission to import anything. I soon found out about all the regulations and to what lengths the ruling clique had gone to keep us out of business.

Like most pilots, I always wondered about what I would do if I failed to pass my next medical examination. I decided I would, as a safety net, start a business I could fall back on should such a misfortune occur. After thinking about it for some time I became convinced there was a definite need in Nassau for an American-type soda fountain.

For months Mary and I explored every aspect of the business. We found a good location and made arrangements to rent space in the Boyle Building in downtown Nassau. Because the space we rented was so small we called the soda fountain "Elbow Room."

I was ready to order the equipment when I discovered that before I could buy a draft in U.S. funds I would first of all have to obtain a licence from Import Control. The Director, Mr. A.K. Cole, flatly refused to consider my application. He quoted a war time regulation restricting new licences to those who had been in business prior to 1940.

Some time after this I had to fly Mr. Wallace Groves, the developer of Freeport, to his Little Whale Cay. Before I left him he said, "Leonard, I heard about your problem with Exchange Control. I think it is disgusting and I have told Stafford (Sir Stafford Sands). Let me have the list of equipment you need and I will arrange to get it for you."

Several weeks later he called to say his boat, the Little Whale Express, would be arriving the following day with my equipment. I could repay him in Bahamian currency at my convenience.

Mary ran the Elbow Room and it was a success right from the start. Her one problem was that she was a soft touch for a sad story and trusted everyone without question.

I was flying more than ever and had little time to help Mary. The first time I dropped by I met the man who had been hired to take our garbage away, something about him made me suspicious so I arranged with Mary to be there when he made his next pick-up.

Right on time he drove up in his truck. I let him load up then I climbed aboard and emptied out all the garbage cans into the truck. Imagine Mary's surprise when she saw only a small amount of garbage in each can. The rest of the space was taken up with ham, bacon, knives, forks–everything except the kitchen sink! We later found out that the garbage man was related to most of the staff.

The pressure of flying an average of over sixty hours a week as well as managing Skyways took its toll on me. I was not getting enough sleep and hated to fly an empty plane. While I had passengers on board I stayed fully alert, but on several occasions on a long flight after I had dropped passengers off and was returning by myself I would fall asleep at the controls. It was frightening to wake up in a screaming dive or on the verge of a stall. Following such incidents I would do everything I could think of to stay awake such as cracking open the window and scooping in the air with my hand, or splashing my face with water.

On one occasion the Ericksons, operators of the Morton Salt Company on Inagua, chartered the Grumman Goose to pick two of them up at Inagua and fly into Cap Haitien, Haiti, prior to flying on to the capital, Port au Prince. I had the Ericksons' word there would be no problem about landing in Cap Haitien. Their agent would be meeting us at the airport.

No sooner had we landed than we were surrounded by barefoot soldiers carrying ancient carbines. I cut the engine off quickly for they were milling around so wildly one

Nigel Marix (left), our marketing manager and I greet passengers as they board a DC-3 in 1950.

126

of them could have walked into the spinning propellers. We were loaded into a dirty open truck and taken to the local gaol where we were held while the Ericksons desperately tried to locate their agent.

Early next morning the agent showed up and we were released on the understanding I would fly into Port au Prince for clearance. On arrival there I had to pay an outrageous sum to customs, immigration, agriculture department, doctor, army, police, airport authority and so on in order to leave. I later found out Dr. Duvalier, the President of Haiti, had been expected to arrive at Cap Haitien the same time as I landed and that the airport had been closed to civil traffic.

There was always something unforeseen happening in the air charter business. I leased a Lockheed 1OA from my friend Dean Franklin of Chalks in Miami to help out with scheduled flights. After an hour on my first flight in this aeroplane, one of the engines cut out for no apparent reason. A few days later I took a full complement of passengers to West End, Grand Bahama in the same aeroplane. On the return flight all I carried was an elderly lady and government mail bags.

I was on a long straight-in approach for runway 090 at Oakes Field with my wheels down when the control tower called and instructed me to go around as there was an aircraft right behind me in trouble which had to make an emergency landing. As I turned to rejoin the circuit my starboard engine cut out and the port engine started firing intermittently. The aircraft could not fly on one engine with the wheels down and the hydraulic motor for pulling the gear up was on the dead engine. The only thing to do was to crank the gear by hand while turning away from downtown Nassau and the populated area and flying towards the southern shore of New Providence in preparation for a crash.

The port engine would clear up for a few minutes and I would gain a little altitude, then when I thought I would be able to get back to the airport the engine would cut out and I would lose altitude. Crossing the southern shoreline almost fifty feet off the water I realised there was no way I could make it back to the airport and I decided to follow my flight instructor's advice: when in doubt, land straight ahead.

I called the control tower and advised them I would be ditching. Fortunately a Pan Am aircraft inbound from Miami was nearby and heard my conversation with the tower. It circled while I landed on the water.

My years of landing seaplanes came into play and the ditching was quite smooth. As soon as the aircraft came to a halt I made my way to the cabin with the intention of getting my lone passenger onto the wing before the plane sank. As I approached the elderly lady with a life vest she complained to me in a very calm voice: "Captain, this ain't Oakes Field."

Despite the pressure I was under I had to smile and wonder at how calm and relaxed she appeared to be. I led her out onto the wing without any problem. I was sure that someone in the South Beach area would have seen me land and soon be on their way to rescue us before the plane sank.

Shortly thereafter one of the company's Grumman Goose seaplanes landed and taxied up to the wing. It was Gil Hensler. He had been returning to Nassau and was about twenty miles away when he heard the conversation between the Pan Am pilot and Oakes Field control tower. He had immediately diverted to my position.

We were able to get the elderly lady aboard through the bow door of the Goose. Gil then clambered out onto the wing of the Lockheed and held the Goose close while I dived back inside to recover the flight log books and the bags of government mail. Then, at Gil's suggestion, we took the anchor out of the Goose and secured the Lockheed in two fathoms of water.

The next day the owner of the aircraft arrived. By then it was on the bottom. It was floated, pulled to the shore near South Beach Road, and the engines and wings were removed. The aircraft was later towed to the docks and shipped to Miami where it was overhauled and later resold. Although only the propeller blades were damaged in the ditching, I was surprised that the F.A.A. would give a certificate of airworthiness to an aeroplane that had been completely submerged in sea water.

Needless to say, I was not on the best of terms with the English manager of Bahamas Airways. He did everything possible to put me out of business. 'Fly With Safety Over the Sea with Four Engines' one of Bahamas Airways advertisements read. Also, a rumour was started that the British Air Registration Board was considering grounding the DC-3. It is still flying to this day, over thirty years later.

The average Bahamian was still not comfortable about flying and the rumours about the DC-3 affected the company severely. I had to discontinue this service and make do with charters only.

CHAPTER 18

TREASURE CAY AGAIN

Some time after the second hotel opened at Treasure Cay, John Rice, a behind-the-scenes type who in my opinion was responsible for the success of Milner Enterprises, started discussions with the Conrad Hilton group to construct a 500 room luxury hotel on a 40 acre beachfront property about half a mile north of the present hotel. After many months of discussions, preliminary plans and an artist's conception of the project were completed. A decision was made to go ahead subject to obtaining a casino licence.

The group involved was already operating a hotel and casino in San Juan, Puerto Rico. They felt that to establish such a resort in a previously unknown place would involve a considerable amount of advertising and promotion. It would be very difficult without a casino.

Personally, I was not in favour of gambling on Abaco, nor did I think government would seriously entertain a request to grant a casino licence to Treasure Cay. Like most Bahamians, I envisaged a honky-tonk Las Vegas-type slot machine palace run by the Mafia. It was suggested that John Rice and I visit the Hilton operation in San Juan for an inspection of the hotel and casino operations there.

I was amazed at how well the operation in San Juan was run and impressed by the high calibre of people attracted to the casino. I returned to Treasure Cay convinced that a casino run by the Hilton group would guarantee the success of the Treasure Cay hotel and would in no way introduce the wrong element into Abaconian society.

Shortly after my return I went to see Sir Stafford Sands, the Minister of Tourism. He had done much to promote tourism in The Bahamas and was overjoyed to hear that such a prestigious group was attracted to Treasure Cay. He agreed to do whatever he could to encourage the investors.

Within a few days I saw him again and he told me it would be a waste of time to apply for a casino licence on Abaco. However, he was sure something could be worked out with Bahamas Amusements of Freeport to amend their licence to take in Abaco.

Several meetings were held between the two groups and an agreement in principle was reached. It proved difficult to get together with Sir Stafford because of the impending 1967 elections. A decision was made to wait until after the election. Needless to say, with the P.L.P. winning the election, that was the end of a project that would have guaranteed the success of Treasure Cay.

For some time Tom Stanley, one of our partners, was very dissatisfied with decisions Dumas pushed through, without consultation, regarding the development. I fully supported Tom and realised how tenuous my situation would have been had I not been a Bahamian minority partner. Eventually, Tom decided to sever his relationship with Dumas.

Before leaving, he apologised to me for having introduced me to Dumas. As a parting gift he transferred his shares to me, much to the annoyance of Dumas.

Not long after this I was notified that Dumas was not well and it might be some time before he could return to Treasure Cay. This was followed by news that his family, doctor and lawyer had declared Dumas incompetent to manage his affairs. As a result, they were anxious to find a buyer for Treasure Cay.

Some time early in 1969 the Dumas interest was sold to a syndicate headed by Deltec Banking Corporation and several merchant banks in London. The syndicate did not buy me out as they were interested in retaining me as Managing Director. Shortly after this I sold fifty percent of my shares to Mr. McKinnon, the owner of Drambuie Liqueurs. He had built the first home on Windward Beach, part of Treasure Cay.

For some time I commuted several times a week between Nassau and Abaco. I had retained a Piper Aztec when I sold Skyways so transportation to and from Treasure Cay presented no problem as I piloted the aircraft myself.

There were always problems, great and small, that I was called on to settle. It seemed these problems always developed just after I had returned to Nassau. Such was the case when I received a call saying there was a problem between two Green Turtle Cay men and a long-serving employee. I wearily returned to Treasure Cay and investigated.

It appeared that the employee had brought two ladies of the night over from Florida who were occupying two rooms in the hotel and doing a brisk business with the local studs. One of the Green Turtle boys had developed a crush on one of the girls. The employee considered the girls to be his private property and an argument had taken place on the pool deck. One of the Green Turtle boys pulled a gun and aimed it at the employee. A tourist standing nearby had pushed him into the pool and the gun discharged into the air harmlessly.

I had the three of them in my office, heard their stories and decided to terminate their services there and then. The ladies of the night were escorted to the airport and returned to Miami. The Green Turtle boys went home heartbroken and the employee took off for Nassau.

About a week later I was summoned to the office of the Minister of Labour, Sir Milo Butler. On arrival I found the employee sitting comfortably with a satisfied smile on his face. I was kept standing for a long time while Sir Milo read his Bible out loud.

Eventually Sir Milo raised his eyes and acknowledged my presence. In a most unfriendly voice he told me, "I am not going to let you take advantage of my black brother." He indicated the employee. "You must apologise and give him his job back."

After some discussion it became clear that Sir Milo was not interested in hearing the truth of the matter, but I could not allow government to run my business on rumours.

"There is no way any of these three men will be hired as long as I am in charge," I told him.

At that, Sir Milo Butler faced me fully and warned: "As long as you are connected with Treasure Cay my government and I will keep it under our thumb, thumb, thumb!!!"

I left his office and went directly to Deltec and reported the meeting. I suggested it would be best for the good of Treasure Cay Limited if I resigned. A few days later my resignation was accepted. That ended ten years of blood, sweat and tears for a dream that had only partially been fulfilled.

CHAPTER 19

POLITICS

On public holidays, Sundays and Fridays, when most of the Nassau business houses closed at midday, many people turned up at the Pan Am building near the Eastern Parade. They were there to see off friends and family departing for Harbour Island or some other Out Island destination or merely to watch the planes take off. Flying was still in its infancy in The Bahamas and it would be some time before the novelty wore off.

Invariably the men at these gatherings got around to politics. So entrenched were the white political leaders that the rising tide of race consciousness, very evident elsewhere in the world, was foolishly ignored.

But a sense of fairness motivated many whites. I remember how pleasantly surprised I was to find that many men felt the same way as I did, and that the leading politicians had to change their attitude towards black and poor white Bahamians.

It was obvious that the division between the races left much to be desired and that The Bahamas was heading for trouble unless attitudes and policies were changed. Perhaps my thinking had been drastically changed by my years in the R.C.A.F.

One of my bunk mates at Stalag Luft III had been Cy Grant, a black Trinidadian hero. We had shared so much in common and I loved him like a brother. I had bragged to him about our beautiful islands. Now I wondered what he would think when he came to visit, as he promised he would.

During one of these heated discussions at the Pan Am site someone came up with the idea of starting a political party for all Bahamians, black and white. Thus the Bahamian Betterment Party was born in Late 1948 or early 1949, the first political party in The Bahamas. I was conscripted and reluctantly agreed to run for one of the Abaco seats in the 1949 election.

Most of our original group were like babes in the woods when it came to politics. No one realised until it was too late that our party had been taken over and manipulated by well-placed representatives of the very same people we felt were destroying The Bahamas. When the election was over the party died a quick and planned death.

Some time during 1952 two of my good friends, Cyril Stevenson and H.M. Taylor, were the leading forces behind the formation of the Progressive Liberal Party. Like the B.B.P., they feared the division between the two races and wished to do something about it.

I seriously considered joining the P.L.P. and had several conversations with Cyril and H.M. in this connection. Fortunately, before I got around to committing myself, I overheard a conversation between several members of the P.L.P. who were preaching racial hatred like I had never heard before. To join them would be jumping out of the cooking pot and into the fire.

I was so concerned I discussed what I had overheard with H.M. a few days later. He readily admitted that he was aware of what was happening but his hands were tied. The racial propaganda was already paying off, especially at the grass roots level. For him to attempt to change the course of events would mean political suicide, he told me.

The P.L.P. won the government and retained power for 25 years by fanning the flames of racial hatred. They took over many private businesses, including Bahamas Air Ways and hotels, and proceeded to overstaff them with supporters, friends and relatives. This was no more than a ploy to control votes and ensure victory at the polls time and time again.

Not long after the P.L.P. came to power they made life so intolerable that H.M. Taylor and Cyril Stevenson had to leave the party they had worked and sacrificed so much to get started. They realised they had created a monster.

In 1955 the Editor of *The Tribune*, Sir Etienne Dupuch, became concerned about the effects of racial propaganda which was sweeping The Bahamas like wildfire, even being voiced from the pulpits of churches. Sir Etienne was a fighter and a man who loved his country. He decided that the best way to fight the political cancer was to start a party in opposition, represented by prominent blacks and whites. So the Bahamas Democratic League was formed.

Unfortunately, it was too late. Gone was the friendliness and trust that had existed between the races for many, many years,

Until the coming of the P.L.P. all members were elected as independents. No salary was received and the term was for seven years. In order to get a project started a member would lobby his parliamentary friends. It was usually a case of "you scratch my back now and I'll scratch yours later."

With the arrival of a well-organised P.L.P. opposition, this approach had to change. As a result the United Bahamian Party was formed in 1956 with all independent members joining the party. I was personally sorry to see the party system take over. It destroyed independent thinking and put power into the hands of ruthless men who controlled the parties and called all the shots. The remainder of the elected members were nothing more than rubber stamps, robots who stood or sat when the button was pushed. I know this was true of the U.B.P. and it seemed even more so in the P.L.P.

All parliamentary members of the U.B.P. would meet for lunch each week at the Fort Montague Beach Hotel, supposedly to conduct the business of the party such as set the agenda and approve members of committees and boards. To me this was a farce as the leaders had already met in secret beforehand and made their choices.

I became very discouraged and had it not been for several members I held in very high regard, particularly Foster Clark, Peter Graham, Fred Brown and Basil Kelly, I would have resigned after the first political luncheon. As it turned out, my days in the party were numbered anyway.

Several members objected to a suggestion that could have been damaging to Eugene Dupuch, the brother of Sir Etienne. A young, pompous member, one of Sir Stafford's prodgeny, accused me of leaking party information to Mr. Dupuch. At the time, I hardly knew Mr. Dupuch and was sure I had not discussed U.B.P. business with him. He later confirmed this.

It was no secret that the waiters and waitresses serving luncheon at the Fort Montague Hotel were all trained listening posts for the P.L.P. and I would assume that leaks, if any, were caused by them. There was never any love lost between the pompous young member and me. I was not surprised when, years later, he became a great contributor to the P.L.P. election campaign fund.

As a result of "the leak" fiasco I resigned from the party and ran as an independent member in the Abaco constituency in the following election. I won by a wide margin and was returned as the Senior Member of the three-member constituency. When it was all over I was surprised I did so well when I considered the enormous amount of money that was spent to defeat me, for I had little money of my own. I did, however, have the use of several large boats donated by friends and an amphibious aircraft.

A few days before the election I flew several of my campaign generals to the settlements they would be working during the election. Before landing we circled the settlements several times throwing out leaflets saying: "GO AND GROW WITH ABACO. VOTE FOR A NATIVE SON - LEONARD THOMPSON."

At the last stop, Coopers Town, I was due to drop off my friend Henry Kinnear, an ex-motor cycle policeman from Nassau who had been born in the Coopers Town area and still had friends and relatives there. Henry was throwing the leaflets out of the window as I circled prior to landing and reminded me not to leave without giving him the cash for expenses. Without a thought I picked up a packet containing 300 pounds and handed it to Henry. In one fluid movement he threw the packet out of the window.

I instantly realised what I had done and for a moment I froze as ten shilling and one pound notes floated down over Fire Road. By the time we landed the word was abroad that Leonard Thompson had dropped thousands of pounds from his aircraft. The following day the police arrived from Nassau to investigate. Luckily, Henry's friends were doing the investigation and they accepted his explanation of the incident. This did not please my opponents who were hoping I would be disqualified from entering the election.

I was elected four times to the House of Assembly, in 1949, 1956, 1962 and 1967. I never did like politics. I was thrust into my first campaign and, circumstances being what they were in the fifties and sixties, I chose to stick with it. I hoped that somehow we would gather enough force among right-thinking members to change the entrenched political reactionaries. Changes did come, but not fast enough.

Winning an election in the Out Islands in those days depended to a great extent on getting the support of the leaders in each settlement of the constituency. The majority of the voters were influenced by their leaders and voted accordingly. In some of the settlements we were handed lists of the voters the leaders said they controlled. On the night before the election,we were told how much each man expected for his vote and this was paid to the leader. I can remember one settlement that had three leaders. I was handed three different lists of guaranteed votes and many of the names submitted appeared on all three lists. By the eve of the election candidates were usually too tired to argue matters and paid up.

The buying of votes and giving of treats during an election was, of course illegal, but it was very fashionable and was openly accepted at the time. Before the coming of the party system the candidate had to bear all costs. In many cases he was so deep in debt by the end of the campaign it would take him years to get out of trouble. I personally know of two gentlemen, Roy Russell and Georgie Knowles, who both represented Abaco, Shortly after, both went broke and lost their businesses. Roy moved to Florida and Georgie died a pauper.

During the days of the P.L.P. government the candidates' expenses were paid for by the Government and they had the party machine behind them. Once elected, many P.L.P. Members of Parliament went from the proverbial rags to riches almost overnight while, apparently, in service of their country.

It was the policy of the leaders in the House of Assembly and government in general not to encourage deficit spending. As a result of this policy there were few major projects undertaken in the Out Islands, with the exception of Harbour Island and Eleuthera. Many of the elected representatives had Harbour Island and Eleuthera roots and this helped these areas to command the lion's share of Out Island spending.

In the past, representatives for Abaco had no ties or attachment to the island. It was a case of "where your treasure is your heart will be also." Unlike present day M.P.s who are paid salaries and benefits, representatives served with no salary and still found time to earn a living. I was able to use my position to meet investors and wealthy individuals and influence them to visit Abaco. Some returned and started major developments such as Murcheson on Spanish Cay and Edwards on Walkers Cay.

In 1949 I met Mr. Maclaren, President of National Container Corporation, and his Vice President Mr. Ed Hobbs. During our brief meeting I discovered both of them were ardent fishermen I invited them to Abaco, promising I would take them fishing if one of them would pull up the anchor. A short while later Mr. Hobbs called to say they would be arriving the following weekend.

This gave me time to contact my old friend, Dewitt Lowe, whom I considered the best fisherman in Hope Town at the time. We arranged to meet him at Cornish Cay on a beautiful day with perfect fishing conditions. Dewitt proved his expertise by guiding us to a wonderful day's fishing that included the largest dog snapper I have ever seen.

From the remarks the executive fishermen made I was sure I had found two more promoters for Abaco. I was not surprised when they came back the next month. During this visit I mentioned that Mr. Wallace Groves was interested in selling his timber lease in Abaco, Grand Bahama and Andros. Later on I flew them into Little Whale Cay

Mr. Dobbs was president of the National Container Corporation. He bought the Bahamas Timber rights which were later absorbed by Owens Illinois. Here he is pictured with our catch–which included a large dog snapper.

where Mr. Groves resided and a deal was made. National Container Corporation of America agreed to purchase all the timber rights and were soon shipping the timber to their Jacksonville operation.

Several years later N.C.C. was absorbed by Owens Illinois. They continued to cut and ship lumber from Pine Ridge, Grand Bahama, to Jacksonville, Florida, where it was pulped and used for paper products. When the trees had all been cut on Grand Bahama the operation was moved to Snake Cay, Abaco, in 1959.

The Owens Illinois operation had a great effect on the development of Abaco. A logging road system of 1600 miles was established and many of these roads are usable to this day. The Great Abaco Highway was constructed and ran from Sandy Point in the south west and Hole in the Wall in the south east to join and extend all the way to Crown Haven in the north. The completion of the highway in 1961 provided access by land between the various Abaco communities for the first time.

The 380-foot Hudson River Luxury Queen Steamer the *Robert Fulton* had been built in 1903. For nearly 50 years it carried honeymooners, tourists and businessmen around Manhattan. In 1950 the N.C.C. found her tied up at a New York wharf waiting to be scrapped. They bought her and had her completely overhauled in Jacksonville. The huge paddle wheels, engines and three smoke stacks were removed. After refurbishing she was towed to The Gap on Grand Bahama where she served as the hub for the timber operations there.

Three years later the *Robert Fulton* was towed to Snake Cay, Abaco, her final resting place. Again she was used as Headquarters for the timber operation. She even provided housing for visiting V.I.P.s. Her four decks encompassed a school room, barber shop, beauty parlour, clinic, dining room, ballroom, motion picture theatre and laundry. The company store on board was the largest supermarket on Abaco and was patronised by residents from all over who could reach her easily by car using the Great Abaco Highway. The *Robert Fulton* was the biggest attraction on Abaco at the time.

CHAPTER 20

POLITICS AND PIGS

For years I kept my family on the verge of bankruptcy because of the financial drain of introducing Abaco to investors and providing many free emergency medical flights from Abaco to Nassau. I look back with some satisfaction that not all of my labours were in vain. Many of the people I introduced to Abaco started major developments such as Murcheson of Spanish Cay, Edwards of Walkers Cay, Owens Illinois, Treasure Cay Limited and, most recently, The Great Abaco Beach Hotel.

Many others became private home owners who built their own homes and later encouraged others to build. No doubt this was the start of the second home owners arrival on Abaco that has grown so much over the years. Today there are over 1200 private homes owned and occupied by these residents. Statistics show that revenue from this source is today estimated to be about 25% of the total revenue generated by all visitors to Abaco. One estimate puts their contribution at 15 million dollars every year.

As manager of Bahamas Air Ways I was able to increase the frequency of scheduled flights from Nassau to Abaco. We went from once a month to once a week to, finally, daily flights. I was severely criticised for this by the two Bahamian Directors, H.G. Christie and Kenneth Solomon, who said I was providing too many flights to Abaco and not enough to Eleuthera. They were reluctant to discontinue the Abaco flights, however, as they proved to be quite profitable.

In the arena of politics I was never accepted by the power block in Nassau, mainly because of my independent thinking. The same can be said for my brothers. Chester contested a seat in Cat Island as an independent and, much later, Montague. Maurice held a senior position in Immigration and crossed one of the ruling elite. Shortly afterwards he was demoted and sent to Mayaguana as a Junior Commissioner, the equivalent of being sent to Siberia in those days.

I was passed over time and time again for appointments which I was well qualified to handle, especially some involving aviation. As time went on there was little doubt left in my mind that the few members who controlled The Bahamas were only interested in Nassau, Eleuthera and Freeport.

Take for example the case of a major oil company that was looking for a large bunkering facility. With my help they carried out intensive investigations to determine the best location in The Bahamas for such an operation. The investigation proved beyond a doubt that the southern end of Abaco was choice number one and Fortune Island, Acklins, the second choice.

A Bahamian company was formed and application to the government to carry out the operation was ready. One year later I was still trying to get this on the agenda of Cabinet. I was not surprised when the company became discouraged and left. Later on I learned that a member of Cabinet put together a syndicate and quickly obtained approval for the present Freeport facility. One Minister was responsible for putting together the syndicate that had no trouble moving into Freeport.

Another good example was the case of Owens Illinois. Shortly after completing the lumber operation on Abaco, in view of the vast amount of equipment, homes and infrastructure that they had built, they looked for something else they could do on the island. After several feasibility studies they decided to start a sugar plantation with a modern sugar refinery south of Marsh Harbour.

When I discovered there was considerable opposition to this plan by prominent members of government, including two of the Abaco Representatives, I arranged a meeting in Nassau at the Garfunkel Auditorium. I invited the Abaco community living in Nassau and, at my own expense, flew in 3O prominent men from the various settlements of the island. The meeting was a fantastic success and the other two Abaco Representatives then went on record as supporting the project. Shortly afterwards, Owens Illinois was given the go-ahead by government.

Most of the Royal Governors who arrived in The Bahamas quickly realised that it was a lot easier to go with the flow of the ruling clique than fight against the many glaring examples of greed and lack of fairness. A few did stand up for right like Sir Robert Neville, a former Brigadier General in the British Marines.

Shortly after his arrival in The Bahamas I had the honour of piloting his aircraft to one of the Out Islands. Following this I was invited to serve as one of his honorary A.D.C.s, wearing my R.C.A.F. uniform on those occasions when I accompanied him on ceremonial duties. This did not

Sir Robert Neville, Governor of The Bahamas from 1950-1953 was an avid outdoorsman.

go down too well with many of the ruling clique. To make matters worse, I was awarded an Order of the British Empire (O.B.E.).

One particular Member of Parliament took special exception to my award. He would often make snide remarks about my association with Sir Robert but I ignored him, putting it down to jealousy. A typical remark was: "I hear you received an O.B.E. You know what that stands for, don't you–Other Bastard's Efforts!"

I could afford to turn the other cheek. There had been a recommendation by the Officer commanding the Florida Coast Guard Station after I had rescued a badly injured sailor from Turks Island at night.

At that time there was no airport and the Coast Guard had found it too rough and dangerous to land a Grumman Albatross. It was arranged that I should land a Grumman Goose on a small cleared area on a salt pan near the town. The Goose did not carry sufficient gasoline for the return trip. I expected to pick up gasoline at South Caicos from the P.A.A. emergency airport. They always had a reserve of regu-

I received the O.B.E. from Sir Robert Neville, which was a great honor.

145

lar gasoline for their ground equipment and I had on several previous occasions been forced to rely on their generosity. Their gasoline did not have the octane rating necessary for high powered aeroplane engines so I took no more than absolutely necessary. Even so, I kept one eye on my cylinder head temperature gauge and my fingers crossed. The low octane rating might have caused overheating of the engine.

I arrived at South Caicos around midnight and was told that their supply ship had been delayed and they were just about out of supplies. I proceeded to Turks Island and landed by the light of parked trucks.

The sailor was suffering from a broken back. He had fallen from his ship onto a barge tied alongside. Jack Ryan, one of our licensed mechanics, had accompanied me on the trip and we discussed the fuel situation. We decided to get as far as Georgetown, Exuma, and assess the situation then.

Over Georgetown I decided to attempt to make it with little or no reserve fuel because the sailor's condition was grim. We were in radio contact with Nassau and I knew I could land on the water if we fell short.

On the final approach to Oakes Field I levelled out and first one and then the other engine cut out completely. I rolled to a stop with fire engines racing alongside.

The injured sailor was transferred to a waiting Coast Guard plane to be taken on to Miami. I left the Goose on the runway and Jack Ryan later fueled it up and taxied to our hangar.

Jack Ryan was an American. He married a Nassau girl, Marie Johnson, and lives there to this day.

The little clique that ruled Nassau were upset with Sir Robert when they failed to have him recalled before his term of office expired. They resorted to many petty intrigues designed to make his tenure of office as unpleasant as possible. Sir Robert ignored them and made several long overdue changes. When he did leave, the majority of Bahamians were sad to see him go.

Sir Robert was a keen sportsman. He loved Scuba diving and water skiing and was extremely active for his age. He was forever asking me to arrange a wild boar hunt on Abaco. So in the end I arranged with an old friend, Maurice Clark of Sandy Point, to meet me on the south coast of Abaco at Cross Harbour.

Maurice had sailed with my father for many years during Prohibition and later hauling lumber from the saw mills of Abaco to Cuba and Tampa. He was a great hunter and had told me this was his favourite hunting ground.

Sir Robert brought along his houseguest, a wartime army friend, and I brought along my brother Joe, who I was teaching to fly. After we landed and anchored the Goose, Maurice came alongside in his boat accompanied by four hunting dogs that were so skinny their bones looked as though they were ready to pop through their skin. I knew Sir Robert well enough to know what was going to happen soon.

The moment we reached land Sir Robert opened his lunch box and fed it to the dogs. This caused Maurice some consternation. He claimed the dogs would hunt better if they were hungry.

We headed out with Maurice and the dogs leading the way followed by Sir Robert and his guest carrying rifles and Joe and I bringing up the rear with 12 gauge shotguns. It was not long before Joe and I decided to leave our guns on the trail and pick them up later.

After an hour or more of covering the roughest terrain one could imagine, the dogs took off barking and we followed them at a run. When we caught up with them they were at the bottom of a pine tree looking up and barking at a large wild cat. Maurice was very upset when we refused to shoot the cat. Personally, I was all in favour of disposing of it but Sir Robert was an Englishman so I kept my opinion to myself. To this day our local ground-nesting parrots, unique in the world, are endangered by feral cats attacking the young at nesting time.

It was difficult to get the dogs away from the cat in the tree but in due course they took off again. We ran, following their barks and the squeal of a pig. After a while it occurred to me we were running in a circle and not gaining on dog or pig. We finally caught up to Maurice trussing a 50 lb. pig.

The moment the pig was firmly tied Maurice whipped out his knife and, with a few swift strokes, castrated the poor beast. As soon as the jewels were off the dogs were fighting over the tasty morsels. Sir Robert was livid. "My good man, how could you do such a cruel thing?" he cried.

"If I don't do that," Maurice told him, "the meat will be rank rank."

After the hog had been killed and the guts disposed of, Maurice loaded it onto his back. Where the four legs were tied together he pulled up to his forehead and set off back towards the aircraft.

Just as we stopped to retrieve our guns the dogs took off again with Maurice right behind them. The rest of us flopped to the ground exhausted and awaited his return. We had all had more then enough of this endurance test set by a man much older than Sir Robert.

Maurice arrived back about an hour later with another hog a little smaller than the first. As a way of greeting I asked him, "How will we ever get these pigs back to the plane?"

"No trouble, boss," he replied. "Dese just two stop hogs."

I only had a vague idea what he meant by "two stop" hogs. Off we went with Maurice in the lead, one hog supported by his forehead and the other carried by hand. I was having trouble just carrying my shotgun.

After a while Maurice called a halt. He placed the pig he was carrying by hand on the ground and hooked the other onto the branch of a tree that looked as if it had been used for the same purpose many times before. He turned to Sir Robert, "Your Worship, das one stop."

After a five minute rest we set off again with Maurice setting such a pace we all had trouble keeping up, particularly Sir Robert's friend. He seemed on the verge of collapse by the time we caught up to Maurice again. "Das two stop," he told us. "Next stop, boat and plane."

And so it was. A ten minute flight took us to Sandy Point where Reuben Dean and his lovely wife Glacie had prepared a sumptuous lunch for us. After lunch, Sir Robert and I walked around Sandy Point while his friend went for a swim. Not long afterwards we were called to the beach where Sir Robert's friend had fainted and was lying unconscious.

We rushed him to the Goose and headed for Nassau where the doctors said he was suffering from heat stroke and exhaustion. He recovered and I'm sure he remembers that two stop hunting trip on Abaco to this day.

CHAPTER 21

INDEPENDENCE FOR ABACO?

Over the years I became more and more disgusted with politics and many politicians. I lost the respect I had for many of my political colleagues. Finally, in 1968, I decided not to offer myself as a candidate again.

Much to my surprise and against my advice, my brother Roscoe decided to contest the seat I was in the process of vacating. Roscoe had always been my campaign manager and without his organisational and financial help I would have had a rough time winning any one of my elections. When it was clear he was determined to run I went all out to help him.

Unfortunately, Roscoe was not as well known in the north of Abaco as he was in the south, where he would have been certain to win. It was because of Roscoe's support that Sherwin Archer won the southern seat by a wide margin.

The P.L.P. was able to secure the help of two white farmers by promising to lease them 5,000 acres of land if they would support their candidate. They were well known in the area and worked hard to secure the lease. As a result, Roscoe lost what would have been a marginal area for a white man to win due to the racial propaganda that had begun to raise its ugly head on Abaco.

For my part, it was great to be out of politics and to concentrate on our various businesses that Mary had been working so hard to hold together–Dirty Dick's, Blackbeard's Tavern, and Thompson Brothers Liquors.

The years flew by and it was almost time for another election. The pressure mounted for me to contest the seat in North Abaco again. This was brought about because the P.L.P. were using independence as an election issue. A vote for the P.L.P. was a vote for independence in the near future.

Many people on Abaco were opposed to this move and, as a result, a petition to Her Majesty Queen Elizabeth II was drawn up and circulated for signatures. The petition requested that, at the time of granting independence to The Bahamas, Abaco would remain a colony of England. In spite of threats and intimidation, 67% of Abaco's residents signed the petition in favour of remaining a colony.

Had the question of independence been put to the nation in the form of a referendum the response would have been an unqualified "no." By tying the issue of independence in with party loyalty to the P.L.P., Prime Minister Pindling forced many staunch liberals who were opposed to independence to go along with him.

During one of my frequent visits to Abaco, Lucien Stratton suggested that we should see Sir Frederick Bennet, a British member of parliament residing on Green Turtle Cay. Sir Frederick had indicated that he wished to meet us and might be able to steer us in the right direction in seeking support for our petition. An appointment was made and Lucien and I went to Green Turtle Cay where Floyd Lowe introduced us to Sir Frederick.

It seemed to me that Sir Frederick was very sympathetic and encouraging. He thought our chances would be greatly improved if we could get Grand Bahama to go along with us. As he put it, geographically it would be a much neater package. He thought we would need the services of a constitutional lawyer and suggested a friend of his, a Mr. Bell, who was also a Member of Parliament. On his return he would discuss the matter with Mr. Bell.

Not long afterwards, Lucien and I received a letter from Mr. Bell stating that he was interested in our cause and would like to come to Abaco to meet us and get a feel of the situation. If he decided to represent the people of Abaco his fees could be discussed at that time. For the time being we would be responsible only for his airfare and accommodations.

On his arrival in Nassau I flew him to Abaco and Grand Bahama and he talked with many of the prominent and influential men. He was extremely optimistic and felt that, due to the political climate in England at that time, our chances of success were very good. They would be greatly diminished, however, if Grand Bahama was not part of the deal.

Before Mr. Bell left Nassau he agreed to represent the Greater Abaco Council, the moving force behind the petition to remain a part of the British Empire. I thought his fees very reasonable and agreed to be responsible for payment. A drive for funds was initiated, but without much success. Throughout my life I have found that the cost of such operations is always borne by a few committed individuals.

In order to further the cause I decided to contest the Coopers Town constituency in the forthcoming election. Right from the start I realised that winning was not going to be an easy task. Gone was the pleasant and friendly relationship that had previously existed between the races on Abaco. So often I heard the sentiment: "Cap, I want to vote for you. You've done so much for me and Abaco." This was followed in a lower voice by: "Don't let the people fool you. This time it's [here the stroke of an outstretched arm] skin for skin."

After my years of involvement in many elections I thought I had seen every trick imaginable deployed by the Bay Street Boys. The things I saw in this election, however, made the Bay Street Boys look like Sunday School teachers. There were many cases of out and out fraud, the most glaring and open being people voting in Freeport then flying over to Grand Cay to cast a second ballot.

Imagine my surprise when, despite all this chicanery, I was declared the winner by 5 votes. A recount made me the loser by 4 votes and a new election was in the cards.

Shortly afterwards, Mr. Bell called me from London. I told him we had lost the election on Grand Bahama, had won one seat on Abaco in the south, and my election was being contested. He replied that, under the circumstances, there was little chance now of the petition being successful.

I decided not to contest the new election for the Coopers Town constituency. The F.N.M. had only seven seats, one of which was held by Errington Watkins in South Abaco. Had I contested the seat and won, it would have had no effect on what the F.N.M. would be able to accomplish. Better, I felt, that Abaco should have one P.L.P. representative who might get government support and funds for the island.

P. O. Box N-1095,
Nassau.

December 22nd. 1972.

The Chairman,
Free National Movement,
Nassau.

Dear Sir,

Kindly accept my resignation as a member of the Free National Movement.

My conscience will not allow me to support a party which has so blatantly ignored the wishes of the electorate, who in good faith elected several members on an anti-Independent ticket.

It would seem to me logical and just that as the Free National Movement members were elected by the anti-Independent sector of the electorate that the party should have maintained an anti-Independent posture, at least to the end of the Conference, thus getting a better deal for the Bahamian people.

The compliant attitude and indeed, complete capitulation of the leaders of the Free National Movement has perpertrated an injustice against the Bahamian people, with which I do not wish to be associated.

Yours faithfully,

Leonard Thompson

Leonard Thompson

In the 1972 election I ran as an FNM candidate. After the election, the FNM altered its position and supported independence. I resigned from the party; this is a copy of my letter.

How wrong my thinking turned out to be. In 25 years of P.L.P. rule, Abaco got practically nothing in return for the millions it contributed to the Treasury.

Some months later, just before the P.L.P. and government leaders were scheduled to go to London to open negotiations towards independence, I was very surprised to receive a call from Mr. Bell. He followed the call with a letter saying he had reason to believe we should proceed with the petition as it now had a good chance of success. We should come to England as soon as possible and bring as many registered voters of Abaco as we could afford.

In short order I had the promise of twelve men from the various settlements who were anxious to go. The provision of round-trip tickets to London and accommodation was just the beginning of the expenses. For the majority of the men we had to provide topcoats, sweaters, hats, shoes and pocket money.

Again I toured Abaco trying to raise money. As usual it was people like Lucien Stratton of Marsh Harbour, Roy Russell of Cherokee Sound, and Roswell Sawyer and Floyd Lowe of Green Turtle Cay who gave most generously. Even so, it was only a drop in the bucket compared to what was needed. We finally obtained a bank loan to finance the cost of taking the delegation to London.

C.R. (Chuck) Hall had shown a keen interest in the cause and had worked very hard with the petition. I was not surprised when he offered to precede the group to London and handle arrangements for accommodation and such.

After many problems and much frustration in getting the delegation to Nassau and ready to depart for London, I discovered one of the party would have to take a flight on the following day. I still had quite a few matters to attend so I decided to take the following day's flight myself.

My eldest son, Leonard Jr., was familiar with London so I arranged for him to go along as a guide and to help in any way he could. This was apparently resented by a few of the delegates. When I arrived two days later I was met at the airport by C.R. Hall. He told me one of the men was behaving in a manner that might bring discredit to Abaco and our delegation.

I called Mr. Bell and he told me we would be presenting our petition to either Mr. Anthony Kershaw or Lord Balneil. He hoped it would be Kershaw as he was known to be sympathetic towards our cause. Lord Balneil was completely opposed.

I discovered that Sir Frederick Bennet's office was in the same building and quite close to Mr. Bell's office. I

TELEPHONE 2-3041

SIR ROLAND SYMONETTE, KT.

P. O. BOX N3709

NASSAU,

BAHAMAS

17th August, 1971

Capt. Leonard M. Thompson
P.O. Box 1095
Nassau, N. P.,
Bahamas.

Dear Capt. Leonard:

Reference attached clipping. To me it is a bit
discouraging, but isn't there something more we can do?
Would it help if Eleuthera and Long Island sent in petitions?

I stand ready to help. Let me know if you think there
is anything I can do.

Sincerely,

Roland Symonette

Sir Roland Symonette

RTS:ar

Sir Roland Symonette, former U.B.P. leader and Premier of the Bahamas, offered his assistance in regard to independence for Abaco.

tried to see him on three or four occasions without success. I finally got the message that Sir Frederick did not want to see me. I learned later from Sir Robert Neville that Sir Frederick had become extremely friendly with Prime Minister Pindling and had changed his mind about helping Abaco.

During the next week I spent many hours with Mr. Bell and Sir Robert Neville. I was introduced to a number of influential people who might help our cause, including three members of parliament. I also contacted the Duke of Hamilton, who owned property at Treasure Cay. He was very sympathetic and agreed to call his brother, Lord Selkirk. I was feeling confident for the feedback I was getting from various sources was very encouraging.

We were, however, having problems with one of our men who was making plans to handcuff himself to the gates of Buckingham Palace. Much to my surprise and consternation, he was being encouraged to do this by our lawyer.

Then bad news struck. Mr. Bell called to say we would be meeting next morning with Lord Balniel.

Right on time we walked into a committee room of the House of Parliament. Our group had to stand against the back wall of a cold, dreary room while Watkins, our lawyer and myself were shown to chairs at a large conference table. Shortly after, Lord Balniel and several male secretaries arrived. Never have I seen such a cold, unfriendly-looking human being. One look and I knew we did not stand a chance.

After we had presented him with the petition and a proposal relating to Great Abaco remaining a colony, Lord Balniel asked us to make our oral presentations. He seemed to be in a hurry.

Errington Watkins started off by reading his prepared text. He was interrupted several times by Lord Balniel who said it was his understanding that the Leader of the Opposition, Mr. Kendal Isaacs, was in favour of independence for all of The Bahamas. Under the circumstances, he told us, we had no right to be there.

Watkins said he had been in the committee room when the vote was taken but had not voted. Lord Balniel pointed out that if he had not voted for it, then he had tacitly voted against it. The argument went on and on and it was obvious that Lord Balniel was trying to discompose Mr. Watkins. It worked. He finally lost his cool and let out a tirade.

After he had cooled off and sat down, I proceeded to read my text. When I had finished, Lord Balniel asked me if I was a friend of Sir Stafford Sands. I replied that I considered myself a very good friend of Sir Stafford's. Lord Balniel shook his head sadly. "He should have told you that we want to be rid of the colonies. Yes, rid of you." With that parting comment, the meeting ended.

I walked with Mr. Bell to his office, just a short distance away. "Is there anything else we can do?" I asked him.

"You can try for another appointment," he told me. "That might take months to arrange. In the meantime, you could demonstrate and get your friend to lock himself to the palace gate. That should get you a lot of publicity. However, I seriously doubt if you will get anywhere with the present government."

I realised it was all over. "If you would be so kind as to let me have your bill to date," I said, "I will settle up tomorrow before I leave for Nassau."

When I returned to our hotel I could hear angry raised voices and my name being mentioned. I entered the room to find Errington Watkins declaring: "Leonard is too old. He doesn't have the guts to fight any more!"

I tried to explain to him that to continue would take a vast amount of money, money we did not have and could not possibly raise. "I am leaving London tomorrow for the Bahamas," I told him. "I hope you will all return with me. The hotel bill will be paid before I leave and after that you are on your own."

The majority did leave with me. Watkins and three or four others stayed on.

I realised before I left Abaco that the majority of our people were not prepared to take any chances physically or financially to seek independence for Abaco. My approach was a one shot try. If it failed, that was that.

It took my brother Chester and me two years to make the final payment to the bank to cover the cost of this exercise.

These gentlemen made up the anti-independence delegation from Abaco that presented a petition to the Governor opposing the P.L.P.'s move for Independence.

CHAPTER 22

RETURN TO ABACO

For thirty-two years I had been a commercial pilot and had at the same time been involved in many projects that kept me busy and constantly on the move. During the latter part of 1977 I found myself with little or nothing to do. For years I had dreamed of returning to Abaco and rebuilding the Great Abaco Club. I had bought this property from its owner, Mr. Walter Blair, in 1967 after a fire had completely destroyed the hotel.

Over the years several developers had made offers for the property with plans for residential development. I felt this would be a great disservice to Marsh Harbour as it was, in my opinion, the only suitable location in the area for a small hotel.

Why not now? I thought. Within a short time I was on my way to Abaco. My greatest problem was to convince Mary to make the move. This was finally accomplished when I decided to sell our beautiful home in Nassau. A month after we had moved and settled in Marsh Harbour Mary was so pleased she claimed it was her idea in the first place.

The hotel was started in late 1977 on the site of the original hotel. There was little or no construction equipment available in Marsh Harbour at the time. I had to import such things as backhoes, cement mixers, and crane and drag line for dredging the proposed marina. None of this had been taken into account when estimating the cost of the development.

The Great Abaco Beach Hotel under construction.

The Great Abaco Beach Hotel shortly after completion.

The hotel consisted of twenty extra large rooms designed with the idea of converting them to "mini suites" later. All the public rooms were large and designed to take care of future expansion of up to 75 or 100 rooms.

After many delays and much frustration we were ready to open in late November of 1979, six months behind our projected completion date. Right from the start the hotel was a success and very popular with the local people. With the help of a staff of 30 we operated the hotel for seven years assisted in various capacities by my daughters Gail, Kathy and Terry, and later my son, Chris.

It had been my hope that my children would take over and run the hotel but, like many parents, I unintentionally tried to live their lives for them. When I discovered that the stress of running a family business was too great I decided to sell. The family members all applauded my decision. They were no doubt relieved to give up working eighteen hours a day, seven days a week.

Not long after our move to Abaco I had been contacted by my old friend Gil Hensler. Gil was a great pilot who had been a test pilot for Grumman Aviation and a transport pilot with the U.S. Air Force. I had brought him to The Bahamas to fly with me at Bahamas Air and later at Skyways. He was anxious to move to Abaco with me and suggested we should start a charter company.

As a result we formed Abaco Air with Joe Muller and Jack Albury as third and fourth partners. Joe was a licensed mechanic and was responsible for the two Piper Aztecs we purchased. Jack ran the booking of the charters and did the accounting. Gil did most of the flying and I helped him on busy days or on his days off. Gil and his wife Lorna moved in next door to us in one of the cottages at the Great Abaco Club. Within a year of starting the company, Gil decided it would be more convenient to have Lorna handle the booking and accounts. As a result, Jack transferred his shares in the company to me and handed over to Lorna. I became more and more involved with the Great Abaco Club and finally withdrew from flying altogether.

For approximately eight years Gil Hensler provided the only locally-based air service on Abaco and was very popular with the Abaco people who knew him. Unfortunately he developed a physical problem that was brought to my attention by several concerned and well-meaning friends who had flown on charters with him. I found an excuse to fly with him and decided that Gil, like all pilots do one day, had reached the point when he should give up flying. It was my sad and difficult task to discuss this with him.

Shortly after this talk, Gil took my advice and grounded himself. He moved to Florida and within a few months died of cancer.

CHAPTER 23

MY FAMILY

My memories would not be complete without mention of my children. Mary and I were blessed with six children, three sons and three daughters.

Leonard Jr. was born shortly after I was shot down over Hamburg. The family had been notified that I was missing in action and felt I would never return. By the time the war was over and I saw him for the first time, Lennie was walking and talking and calling Roscoe "Papa." Over the years all of our children have referred to Roscoe as Papa, a title he enjoys and encourages.

Lennie's first marriage to Anne Maura gave us our first grandchild, Tina. Tina Thompson Scott lives in Nassau with her children, Sasha and Conor. Lennie moved to the U.S. 25 years ago and married Patricia Fusco. They live in Florida and have three children, Lennie III, Laura and Lisa.

Gail arrived one year after I returned from the war. Ironically, she married Gosta Schafer from Hamburg. They have two daughters, Jessica and Diana. Jessica married Ron Wallace and is expecting a son in December 1995. Diana married Chuck Wightman. They all live in Florida.

Jeffrey Thompson

Then followed Jeffrey who, sad to say, lost his life on a diving trip near Freeport at the age of 24. He had just graduated from the University of Tampa and moved to Freeport. Only those who have lost a child can know what Mary and I suffered.

Next to arrive was Kathy, who married Danny O'Kelleher from England. They had one daughter, Monique. Kathy and Monique now reside in Marsh Harbour.

Mary and Leonard, 1950.

Following Kathy was Theresa (Terry). She married Brent Curry. They had one son, Darvin. Shortly after Darvin was born, Brent lost his life in a car accident. Terry lives nearby and is a great help to Mary and I as we grow older and need a helping hand in managing our affairs.

We were surprised when seven years after Terry's birth, Chris arrived, the only child not born at home. He married Peggy Biggs, a classmate from the University of Central Florida. They have two daughters, Jade and Shannon, and are expecting a son in March 1996. They live in Hope Town–near enough for me to enjoy spoiling the kids. Chris and Peggy are both very active in running their Hope Town Hideaway Resort and Real Estate Agency.

Finally, I want my children to know that, during the long years of struggle and adventure, I sought to provide them with advantages I never had. Their appreciation of this brings me joy.

I am now fully retired on Abaco. Mary and I enjoy some quiet times with lots of visits from friends and family. Our children are busy with their lives but stay in constant contact.

I fish and I smoke an occasional fine cigar, but retirement doesn't really suit me. I don't enjoy puttering around the house or garden. I have stayed busy recently helping Chris with his rental villas and real estate business as well as writing this book. Sometimes I am referred to as the "gopher" as in "Leonard, gopher this" and "Leonard, gopher that."

Mary hasn't stopped either. She still cooks for the family as though all the children were home and she loves our frequent and varied company.

As I near the end of this short chapter of my life I ask myself what I would do differently if I had my life to live over again. The one thing I regret is not having been with my children more. I have enjoyed watching some of my grandchildren grow up under my own roof but with my own children I was so busy with overloaded work schedules that I often didn't see them for days or weeks on end.

In 1962 the Thompson family consisted of myself, Lennie Jr., Gail, Jeff, Mary, Kathy, and Terry. Chris was born one year later in 1963.

The last words I would like to pass down to my children, grandchildren, and their children's children is that they should always be honest, fair and true. If they believe in a dream and try to achieve it with hard work and perseverance, all things are possible.

Yes, I believe I am pleased with my life.

POSTSCRIPT

It has not been easy for me to write my memoirs. I was encouraged by the fact that my father and his father lived in a wonderful time and told fantastic stories, but all I can remember are bits and pieces. I wanted my children and the generations to come to have more.

Several professional writers suggested a sensational set of disclosures for commercial use, but my intention in writing this brief account was to share some of my life and experiences with my successors. I am deeply indebted to my friend, Jack Hardy, for his help and support.

This book is dedicated to my wife, Mary, and to the memory of our son, Jeffrey.

My Mary has given me over fifty years of true love and happiness. Our son Jeffrey was with us for only twenty-four years. We had barely gotten to know him when he was taken from us. Son, we have missed you so much.

November 1995

Appendix A - Selected Portions of Pilot's Log Book of Leonard M. Thompson

YEAR 1944		AIRCRAFT		PILOT, OR 1ST PILOT	2ND PILOT, PUPIL OR PASSENGER	DUTY (INCLUDING RESULTS AND REMARKS)	SINGLE-ENGINE AIRCRAFT				MULTI-ENGINE AIRCRAFT					PASS-ENGER
							DAY		NIGHT		DAY			NIGHT		
MONTH	DATE	Type	No.				DUAL (1)	PILOT (2)	DUAL (3)	PILOT (4)	DUAL (5)	1ST PILOT (6)	2ND PILOT (7)	DUAL (8)	1ST PILOT (9)	2ND PILOT (10)	(11)
						TOTALS BROUGHT FORWARD	36:55	31:10	2:30	:15	103:40	44:30	50:10	20:10	71:20	5:05	13:15
MARCH		LANCASTER	Z	S/LDR AVANT	SELF	OPS ON ESSEN SUCCESSFUL											
						9 LOST									5:15		5:15
	27	LANCASTER	P	SELF	HOPENFTELL W/O CUFF SGT MERRITT SGT TARPLEY	X-COUNTRY - BOMBING LANDED AT TOPCLIFF									5:00		
	30	LANCASTER	O	P/O BERRY	SELF	OPS NUORNBERG 1X500-15 CANS											
						BADS FIGHTER COMBATS!! 96 LOST									7:50		
						"GARTH" MISSING											
	31	LANCASTER	Q	SELF	HOSTETLER SGT CUFF W/O FENWICKALL SGT LOCK " MERRITT " TARPLEY	BULLS EYE											
						LANDED A.S.L. U/S									4:30		
						SUMMARY FOR MARCH											
						UNIT 426 SQDN											
						DATE APRIL 1ST 1944											
						A/C TYPE LANC II											
						SIGNATURE M. L. Thompson									9:30	13:05		
						McC/F/L							aerobatics, etc.				
						F/O O.C.B FLIGHT							O.C #426 SQDN				
APRIL		LANCASTER	F	SELF	F/O HOSTETLER F/O FENWICKALL F/O CLIFF SGT LOCK " TARPLEY " MERRITT	BULLS EYE DAY						2:35					
						TOTALS CARRIED FORWARD	36:65	31:10	2:30	:15	103:40	47:05	50:10	20:10	80:50	18:10	18:12

GRAND TOTAL [Cols. (1) to (10)] ... Hrs. ... Mins.

YEARS

168

YEAR 1944	AIRCRAFT Type	No.	PILOT, OR 1ST PILOT	2ND PILOT, PUPIL OR PASSENGER	DUTY (INCLUDING RESULTS AND REMARKS)	SINGLE-ENGINE AIRCRAFT DAY Dual	Pilot	NIGHT Dual	Pilot	MULTI-ENGINE AIRCRAFT DAY Dual	1st Pilot	2nd Pilot	NIGHT Dual	1st Pilot	2nd Pilot	PASSENGER
					TOTALS BROUGHT FORWARD	36.55	81.10	2.30	—.15	103.40	147.05	50.10	30.10	80.20	18.10	13.15
April 14	LANCASTER	"Z"	SELF	CREW	BOMBING DAY						.55					
15		"Z"	SELF	CREW	BOMBING NIGHT										.45	
17	LANCASTER	"Z"	SELF	CREW	BOMBING D.N.C.O. PRT NTER IcKED UP						1.00					
17	LANCASTER	"N"	SELF	CREW	X-CTY BOMBING (B.A.T Confin) 45									3.20		
18	LANCASTER	"Q"	SELF	CREW	OPS PARIS 9X1000 7X500 RRYds NOISY Le Sec V/s GOOD NO CLOUDS 14 LOST									5.20		
22	LANCASTER	"K"	SELF	CREW	OPS DUSSELDORF 1X2000-3 Cans GOOD HAT PRANG, CLEAR. BASE SEARCHLIGHTS & FIGHTERS!! VAPOR TRAILS. GOOD TRIP H.R.Lost									6.20		
24	LANCASTER	"M"	SELF	CREW	OPS KARLSRUHE 1X2000-18 Cans DIFFICULT FLYING-A.S.I. U.S. ARRIVED EARLY GOOD PRANG FEW FIGHTERS 30 LOST									6.45		
26	LANCASTER	"M"	SELF	CREW	OPS ESSEN 1X2000-18Cans CLEAR. BASE SEARCHLIGHT "CONÉ" 39 LOST									4.55		
27	LANCASTER	"M"	SELF	CREW	OPS FRIEDRICHSHAFEN 1X500-14 Cans. INTENSE FLAK GOOD PRANG - 36 LOST SHORT PETROL. LANDED "FORD"									7.25		
				GRAND TOTAL [Cols. (1) to (10)] Hrs.	TOTALS CARRIED FORWARD	36.55	81.10	2.30	—.15	103.40	149.00	50.10	30.10	114.40	18.10	13.16

169

| YEAR 1944 | AIRCRAFT | | PILOT, OR | 2ND PILOT, | DUTY | SINGLE-ENGINE AIRCRAFT | | | | MULTI-ENGINE AIRCRAFT | | | | | | PASS-ENGER |
MONTH DATE	Type	No.	1ST PILOT	OR PASSENGER	(INCLUDING RESULTS AND REMARKS)	DAY DUAL (1)	DAY PILOT (2)	NIGHT DUAL (3)	NIGHT PILOT (4)	DAY DUAL (5)	DAY 1ST PILOT (6)	DAY 2ND PILOT (7)	NIGHT DUAL (8)	NIGHT 1ST PILOT (9)	NIGHT 2ND PILOT (10)	(11)
					TOTALS BROUGHT FORWARD	26.55	31.10	2.30	-.15	103.40	49.10	52.10	30.10	114.40	18.10	13.15
April 21	LANCASTER	"M"	SELF	CREW	FORD TO BASE						1.25					
April 29	LANCASTER	"M"	SELF	CREW	B.A. AT CONTROLS 45 / LOCAL BOMBING - S.B.A. HOMINGS						1.45					
April 30	LANCASTER	"K"	SELF	CREW	AIR TO AIR AND BOMBING / S.B.A. - HOMINGS		2				2.00					
					SUMMARY FOR APRIL											
					UNIT 426 SQDN						9.40			33.50		
					DATE MAY 1ST 1944 A/C TYPE LANC II											
					SIGNATURE ___ M L Haughton											
					O.S ___ /											
					O.C "B" FLIGHT											
May 7	HALIFAX III	"O"	F/L PATTERSON	SELF & CREW	LOCAL DUAL					1						
May 7	HALIFAX III	"O"	SELF	CREW	CIRCUIT & BUMPS						.30					
May 9	HALIFAX III	"Y"	SELF	CREW	X-CTY MAG LGT O- B.A. AT CONTROLS						5.46					
May 10	HALIFAX III	"W"	SELF	CREW	AIR TEST						.35					
May 10	HALIFAX III	"L"	SELF	CREW	X-CTY									3.45		
May 11	HALIFAX III	"P"	SELF	CREW	AIR TO AIR S.B.A. HOMINGS						1.20					
May 20	HALIFAX III	"R"	SELF	W/C HAMBER CREW	NIGHT X-CTY									3.25		
					GRAND TOTAL [Cols. (1) to (10)] 557 Hrs. 05 Min. TOTALS CARRIED FORWARD	26.55	31.10	2.30	.15	104.15	62.21	52.10	30.10	125.10	18.10	13.15

1944 MONTH DATE	AIRCRAFT Type	No.	PILOT, OR 1ST PILOT	2ND PILOT, PUPIL OR PASSENGER	DUTY (INCLUDING RESULTS AND REMARKS)	SINGLE-ENGINE DAY Dual (1)	Pilot (2)	NIGHT Dual (3)	Pilot (4)	MULTI-ENGINE DAY Dual (5)	1st Pilot (6)	2nd Pilot (7)	NIGHT Dual (8)	1st Pilot (9)	2nd Pilot (10)	PASSENGER (11)
					TOTALS BROUGHT FORWARD	46:56	31:10	2:30	.15	104:15	162:20	50:10	30:10	121:10	18:10	13:15
May 22	Halifax III	"R"	Self	F/O Hostetler, F/O Cuff, Sgt Thapley, " Lock, " Merritt	OPS Le Mans 18 x 500									4:45		
					Vis Good Aft Late. Good Prang Taken											
May 23	Halifax III	"P"	Self	Crew Merritt	Local Bombing S.B.A						1:20					
					82 Lost											
					"G" Horings											
May 24	Halifax III	"M"	Self	F/O Hostetler, F/O Cuff, Sgt Thapley, " Lock, " Merritt	OPS Trouville 18 x 500									3:35		
					Easy Trip - No Park. No S/L											
May 25	Halifax III	"R"	Self	Crew Hostetler, " Fentrell, " Cuff, Sgt Lock, " Merritt	Local Bombing Fighter Aff						1:20					
May 27	Halifax III	"R"	Self	Hostetler, Cuff, Lock, Merritt, Thapley	OPS Bourg Leopold 16 x 500									5:05		
					Marrate Lidt Flak - Bros Fighter											
					Kansais 27 Lost - Diverted - Barford St John											
May 28	Halifax III	R	Self	Crew Hostetler, " Fentrell, " Cuff, Sgt Lock, " Merritt, " Thapley	Barford St John To Base						1:45					
May 31	Halifax III	"R"	Self	Hostetler, Cuff, Merritt, Thapley	OPS Au Fevre 18 x 500									3:55		
					Weather Bad. Rain't Trenches Sft											
					All Blood-Track											
				Summary For May Unit 426 Sqdn							11:35			23:50		
				Date June 1st 1944 O/C Halifax III Signature ...... W/C Thompson												
					TOTALS CARRIED FORWARD	46:56	31:10	2:30	.15		50:10			121:10		

1944 Month / Date	Aircraft Type	No.	Pilot, or 1st Pilot	2nd Pilot, Pupil or Passenger	Duty (Including Results and Remarks)	Single-Engine Day Dual	Single-Engine Day Pilot	Single-Engine Night Dual	Single-Engine Night Pilot	Multi Day Dual	Multi Day 1st Pilot	Multi Day 2nd Pilot	Multi Night Dual	Multi Night 1st Pilot	Multi Night 2nd Pilot	Passenger
					TOTALS BROUGHT FORWARD	8:10		8:20	—:15	109:50	235:40	50:10	30:40	235:40	18:10	13:45
June 1																
June 2	Halifax III	"R"	Self	F/O Hostetler / F/O Fentinell / F/O Cuff / Sgt Tradley / Sgt Lock / Sgt McArmitt	OPS Neufchatel 18 x 500 — Clear over target — good prang									5:20		
4	Halifax III	"W"	Self	Crew	Local Flying						:40					
5	Halifax III	"R"	Self	Crew	Base — Scarlesbury						:40					
6	Halifax III	"L"	Self	F/O Hostetler / F/O Fentinell / F/O Cuff	Scarlesbury — Base						:26					
6	Halifax III	"Y"	Self	F/O Cuff / Sgt Tarpley	OPS Houlgate 7x1000 — 6x500. Severe icing on first part of trip. Good prang (M.S.L. u/s)									4:50		
7	Halifax III	"P"	Self	F/O Hostetler / Fent-Bell / Lock / Tarpley / Merritt	OPS Achères									5:05		
8	Halifax III	"P"	Self	F/O Hostetler / Fentinell / Cuff / Sgt Lock / Tarpley / Marritt / Crawford	OPS Mayenne 16x500. Rain and cloud all trip. Good prang. Bombed Newtownards (killed), short of petrol									6:20		
9	Halifax	"P"	Self	Crew	Newtownards to Base						:45					
12	Halifax III	"Y"	Self	F/O Hostetler / F/O Fentinell / F/O Cuff / Sgt Lock / Marritt / Tarpley	OPS Cambrai									4:35		
13	Halifax III	"Z"	Self	Crew	OPS Boulogne 9x1						3:44					
					TOTALS CARRIED FORWARD	8:10		8:20	—:15	110:05	241:15	50:10	30:40	262:40	18:10	13:45

GRAND TOTAL [Cols. (1) to (10)]
600 Hrs. ___ Mins.

| YEAR | | AIRCRAFT | | PILOT, OR 1ST PILOT | 2ND PILOT, PUPIL OR PASSENGER | DUTY (INCLUDING RESULTS AND REMARKS) | SINGLE-ENGINE AIRCRAFT | | | | MULTI-ENGINE AIRCRAFT | | | | | | PASS-ENGER |
MONTH	DATE	Type	No.				DAY DUAL (1)	DAY PILOT (2)	NIGHT DUAL (3)	NIGHT PILOT (4)	DAY DUAL (5)	DAY 1ST PILOT (6)	DAY 2ND PILOT (7)	NIGHT DUAL (8)	NIGHT 1ST PILOT (9)	NIGHT 2ND PILOT (10)	(11)
						TOTALS BROUGHT FORWARD	65	91:10	2:20	15	104:50	173:10	50:10	30:10	142:40	18:10	13:15
	15	Halifax III	"Z"	Self	F/O Hostetler " Fentrell " Cuff Sgt Lock " Merritt " Tarpley	OPS Sterkrade (Ruhr Valley) Bomb Load 16 x 500 - Deep Fighter Cocktails-Intense Light & Heavy Flak Four Jerry Fighters Sighted— Harry Jeffy & Kirk missing									4:50		
						2 Lost		A.B.									
June	19	Halifax VII	"R"	Self	Crew	Air Test						:40					
	20	Halifax VII	"R"	Self	P/O Becker Crew	Fighter Affiliation						:40					
	21	Halifax VII	R	Self	Crew	OPS st Martin						4:15					
				Summary for June								11:50			29.00		
				Unit 426 Sqdn													
				Date July 1st 1944													
				Signature ___ W.L.Thompson													
				O.C. 'B' Flight													
July	1	Halifax VII	"T"	Self	Crew	OPS Biennais						3.50					
July	2	Halifax VII	"V"	Self	F/O Hostetler " Longley " Youngs " Fowlton Sgt Lock	Air Test						:30					
July	4	Halifax VII	"R"	Self Sgt Lane	Crew	OPS Biennais						3:50					
				GRAND TOTAL [Cols. (1) to (10)]		TOTALS CARRIED FORWARD	80:10	2:20	15								

E.L. Blansher W/Cdr.
O.C. 426 Sqdn.

Year		Aircraft		Pilot, or 1st Pilot	2nd Pilot, Pupil or Passenger	Duty (Including Results and Remarks)	Single-Engine Aircraft Day Dual (1)	Day Pilot (2)	Night Dual (3)	Night Pilot (4)	Multi-Engine Aircraft Day Dual (5)	Day 1st Pilot (6)	Day 2nd Pilot (7)	Night Dual (8)	Night 1st Pilot (9)	Night 2nd Pilot (10)	Pass. enger (11)
Month	Date	Type	No.														
						Totals Brought Forward	36:55	3:10	2:30	:15	104:20	206:55	50:10	80:10	147:30	18:10	18:15
July	5	Halifax VII	"R"	Self	Crew	OPS Cahne					44:50	3:25	53:70	50:10	147:30	18:10	18:15
						Diverted Newmarket											
July	6	Halifax VII	"R"	Self	Crew	Newmarket To Base					1:00					
	7	Halifax VII	"P"	Self	Crew	Air Test					:30					
July	7	Halifax VII	"R"	Self	Crew	OPS Bichave-das					4:20					
	8	" "	R	Self	Crew	M.S					2:45					
	27	" "	N	Self	Crew	Formation X Country					1:50					
	29	" "	L.W	Self	Flo Harm Crew	OPS Hamburg					OUTSTANDING					
					Summary For July												
					Unit 426 Squadron						2:00						
					Date July 30c 1944												
					Signature												
						after bombing target					shot down by heavy flak						ore
					R.J.Catheron Sk												
					O C B Flight						Roy Burgess S2						
				GRAND TOTAL [Cols. (1) to (10)]		Totals Carried Forward	36:55	3:10	2:30	:15	104:20	206:55	50:10	14:30	147:30	18:10	18:15
		64 Hrs. 20															

Appendix B -

Selected Portions of P.O.W. Diary
of Leonard M. Thompson

A WARTIME LOG

FOR

BRITISH PRISONERS

Gift from
THE WAR PRISONERS' AID OF THE Y. M. C. A.
37, Quai Wilson
GENEVA — SWITZERLAND

My diary is a standard issue Swiss Red Cross P. O. W. diary. Note on the next page that my initials are reversed. I had to reverse them because the Royal Canadian Air Force reversed them on my first payroll check. When I complained, the paymaster said I would have to wait for the money and fill out a lot of "red tape." We both decided I would stay Maurice Leonard Thompson on pay day, and this mistake followed me throughout the war.

KRIEGE No 6965

THIS BOOK BELONGS TO

F/Lt M. W. Thompson. J86464
R.C.A.F.
P.O.B 943 Nassau N.P.
Bahamas West Indies

Y.M.C.A.

F - <u>28-7-44</u> 1:30 AM <u>The chop.</u> - landed in a forest, face and neck badly burned, no shoes = commenced walking
<u>5:00 A.M</u> - 10:00 A.M Slept in woods
<u>11:00AM</u> Captured by very old man from R.R. Station - too weak tired and sick to resist - taken to local village
1:00 P.M Collected by local police
<u>18:00</u> Hrs Taken to local Luftwaffe near LUBECK. in my first German prison cell face and neck bothering me terribly, no treatment yet

S - 29-7-44 Very uncomfortable night - no bed and boards teeming with lice and fleas
10:00 Jewetrell arrived in room opposite
16:00 Hrs Face and neck bandaged up.
Food so far three slices of dark bread and water

S - 30-7-44 15:00 Hrs "Heron" brought in, for the first time since being captured

M-31-7-44   Left prison during early hours Herron & Fentrell with me also three guards, destination unknown. Train very crowded, have been heading in a westerly direction since starting. country side very beautiful. 18:00 Arrived at interrog center (30 MILES N.E. FRANKFURT. Put in cooler after minor interrogation

T-1-8-44   10:00 AM Face & neck dressed properly Food again - three slices bread and one plate of porridge (around 18:00 HRS)

W=2-8-44   NiL (in all)

T.3-8-44   Interrogated by Lt Schunn

F.4-8-44   Cooler very browned off. can't sleep at night for fleas & lice

S 5-8-44   Interrogated again

S 6-8-44   NiL (in all)

M 7-8-44   18:00 HRS Told by Lt Schunn would be moving also three of crew confirmed dead
1900 HRS moved over to a camp met Rusty Alf. and Gas. Fountain Pen, Watch, and comb returned to me.

T-8-8-44   7 AM On our way to DULAG LUFT 40 MILE journey

5 PM arrived - my first shower since taken prisoner, boy oh boy". Given an amazing Red Cross case with just about every thing in it. God bless the red cross, don't know what we would do with out them. Had a good meal, fed better than any time since 28-7-44 Wrote Card to Mary

W 9-8-44   Spent all day sun bathing - Most of prisoners on camp are American Col Stark (U.S.A) Senior officer of camp

TH 10-8-44   8 AM told moving to Stalag III near Sagan

5:30 PM Movement commenced walked to station - In Italian carriages wooden seats - 10 men to a compartment only seats for six - Uncomfortable night

F 11-8-44   All day on train, plenty of food from RED CROSS parcel

4

S 12-8-44　14:00 hrs arrived at SAGAN. marched to camp. Americans are staying here, but told we are moving on to another camp 1600 hrs commenced march to our camp.
20:00 hrs Arrived at STAMMLAGER LUFT 3. Prison camp. Met Jucy, Labbie, Desrosiars, Tom, Al Bakus. assigned to Block #6 Room 14

S 13-8-44　Spent entire day sun bathing and resting all the old prisoners look very fit, moral is high and every body expect to be back in Eng for Xmas. Food is much better than I expected. all our food is made up from Red Cross parcels, with out these we would definately starve to death.
Mailed a post card to Mary to day — We are only allowed 3 letters and 4 Post cards per month.

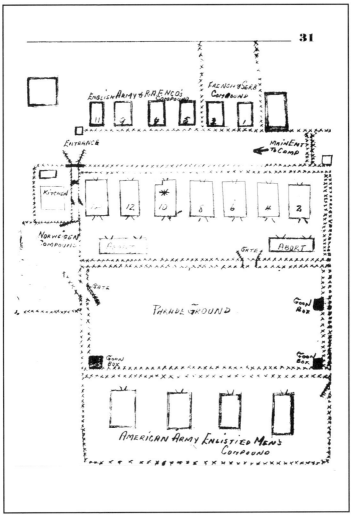

Luckenwalde

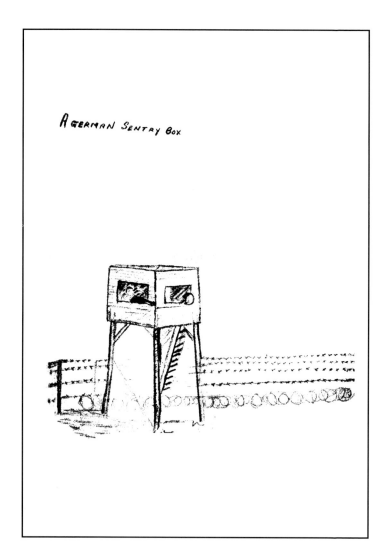

A GERMAN SENTRY BOX

BED 1   F/O BASIL MURRAY

" 2   "   MAC QUEEN

" 3   LT CHRIS MEINTJES

" 4   F/O   LAWLESS

" 5   " SANDERSON MILLER

" 6   " RON WALKER

" 7   P/O GEORGE CHAPMAN

" 8   " JACK McWILLIAMS

" 9   F/LT ALFRED SMITZ

" 10   F/LT LEONARD THOMPSON (SELF)

" 11   F/O JOCK ELLIOTT

" 12   " RAY WATTS

EVEN No's BOTTOM BED
ODD No's TOP BED
Beds are double decker, made of wood, with wooden
slats placed across bed for straw filled sack to lie on

PLAN OF OUR ROOM No 14 SITE 6

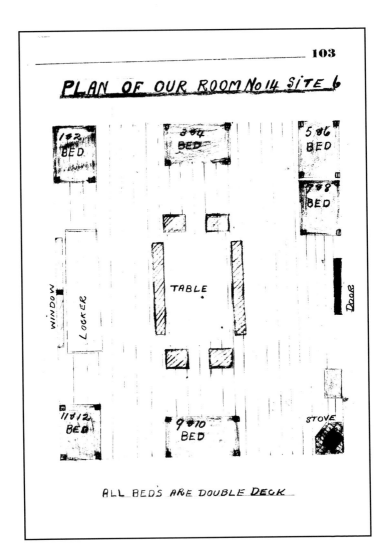

ALL BED'S ARE DOUBLE DECK

Appendix C -

Selected Other Documents

Nr: 0769

Oflag Luft 3

Sagan-Belaria, den _____

PAROLE:

I give my parole as a British Officer / ~~Warrant Officer / N.C.O.~~ that on every occasion I use the new Sports Field to the West of this Camp, I will **not**:

1. Attempt to escape.
2. Make any preparations for future escapes.
3. Have ~~any~~ dealings with other persons outside the fences.

This card is strictly personal, and I understand that any misuse will be considered as an infringement of my parole.

ere Merkmale: _____ _Lt. M. L. Thompson_

Rank and Name

P. O. W. Number _____

185

ROYAL CANADIAN AIR FORCE
OVERSEAS
426   (R.C.A.F.)   SQUADRON

July 31, 1944.

Dear Mrs. Thompson:

Before you receive this letter you will have received
a telegram informing you that your husband, Flight Lieutenant
Maurice Leonard Thompson, is missing as the result of air operations.
I deeply regret that it will take so long for the few details that
are available to reach you for I know how great must be your anxiety.

Your husband and his crew were detailed along with other
members of the Squadron to carry out an attack on enemy installat-
ions at Hamburg, Germany. They took off at 10.22 p.m. on the night
of the 28th July 1944, and set course for the target. Unfortunately
nothing further has been heard from any member of the crew since
time of take-off, although this is not unusual as wireless silence
is always maintained on such sorties.

There is always the possibility however, that your
husband and the other members of his crew may be prisoners of
war, in which case you will either hear from your husband direct,
or from the Air Ministry, who will have been notified by the
International Red Cross Society. In the meantime your husband's
personal effects have been gathered together and forwarded to
the Royal Air Force Central Depository, where they will be held
until better news is forthcoming, or in any event for a period of
at least six months, before being forwarded to you, through the
Administrator of Estates, Ottawa.

The loss of your husband was sustained with great regret
by the members of this Squadron. He was one of our most capable
and experienced pilots, having completed twenty-three sorties over
enemy territory. He was very popular with the personnel of this
Squadron, and particularly with the members of his own crew. I
can say personally that he set a splendid example to all ranks,
and his loss is being felt very keenly.   ......over

On behalf of the entire Squadron I would like to take this opportunity to tender to you our sincere sympathy in your great anxiety, and to join with you in the heartfelt hope that better news will be forthcoming soon.

In closing I would like to assure you that any further information received regarding your husband will be immediately communicated to you. In the meantime if there is anything further you wish to know and which I may have overlooked in this letter, please do not hesitate to write to me, Mrs. Thompson.

Yours very sincerely,

Wing Commander, Commanding,
No.426 (R.C.A.F.) Squadron,
R.C.A.F.   OVERSEAS.

Mrs. M.L. Thompson,
Box 943 Naussau, N.P.
Bahamas, West Indies.

ADDRESS REPLY TO:

THE SECRETARY,
DEPARTMENT OF NATIONAL DEFENCE FOR AIR,
OTTAWA, ONTARIO.

OUR FILE...... R53865 ....(R.0.4)

REF. YOUR ....

DATED ....

ROYAL CANADIAN AIR FORCE

A I R M A I L   OTTAWA, Canada, 8th August, 1944.

Mrs. M.L. Thompson,
Box 943,
Nassau NP Bahamas,
British West Indies.

Dear Mrs. Thompson:

It is with deep regret that I must confirm our recent telegram informing you that your husband, Flight Lieutenant Maurice Leonard Thompson, is reported missing on Active Service.

Advice has been received from the Royal Canadian Air Force Casualties Officer, Overseas, that your husband, and the entire crew of his aircraft failed to return to their base after taking off to carry out bombing operations over Hamburg, Germany, on the night of July 28th and the early morning of July 29th, 1944.

The term "missing" is used only to indicate that his whereabouts is not immediately known and does not necessarily mean that your husband has been killed or wounded. He may have landed in enemy territory and might be a Prisoner of War. Enquiries have been made through the International Red Cross Society and all other appropriate sources and I wish to assure you that any further information received will be communicated to you immediately.

Attached is a list of the members of the Royal Canadian Air Force who were in the crew of the aircraft together with the names and addresses of their next-of-kin. Your husband's name will not appear on the official casualty list for five weeks. You may, however, release to the Press of Radio the fact that he is reported missing, but not disclosing the date, place, or his unit.

Your husband was promoted to the rank of Acting Flight Lieutenant with effect from June 15th, 1944.

Permit me to extend to you my heartfelt sympathy during this period of uncertainty and I join with you and the members of your family in the hope that better news will be forthcoming in the near future.

Yours sincerely,

R.C.A.F. Casualty Officer,
for Chief of the Air Staff.

R.C.A.F. G. 32B
500M—1-44 (3778)
H.Q. 885-G-3213

188

ROYAL CANADIAN AIR FORCE

OTTAWA, Canada, 30th August, 1944.

Mrs. M.L. Thompson,
Nassau N.P., Box 943,
Bahamas, B.W.I.

Dear Mrs. Thompson:

Confirming my telegram of recent date,
advice has been received from the International Red
Cross Society, quoting German information which states
that your husband, Flight Lieutenant Maurice Leonard
Thompson, is now a Prisoner of War.

It is a pleasure to convey this further
information as I feel it will relieve to some extent the
great anxiety endured by you and the members of your family.

Attached is a leaflet giving particulars of
Departments and Organizations from whom you can obtain advice
and assistance, together with a few notes regarding personal
effects, promotions etc.

May I again assure you that any additional details received at these Headquarters will be communicated to
you immediately.

Yours sincerely,

W. M. Wismer S/o

R.C.A.F. Casualty Officer,
for Chief of the Air Staff.

R.C.A.F. G. 32B
500M—1-44 (1778)
H.Q. 885-G-32B

189

Chris Thompson, youngest son of Leonard and
Mary (born 1963), shown here as a student and
young pilot.

Index

I

J

K

L

M

Notes